THE COMPLETE
SLOW COOKER
COOKBOOK

ESSENTIAL RECIPES FOR HEARTY AND DELICIOUS CROCKERY MEALS, MENUS, AND MORE

WENDY LOUISE

SOURCEBOOKS, INC.
NAPERVILLE, ILLINOIS

Published by Sourcebooks, Inc.
P.O. Box 4410, Naperville, Illinois 60567–4410
(630) 961–3900
Fax: (630) 961–2168
www.sourcebooks.com

Originally published in 2003 by Champion Press, Ltd.

Library of Congress Cataloging-in-Publication Data
Louise, Wendy.
The complete slow cooker cookbook : essential recipes for hearty and delicious crockery meals, menus, and more / by Wendy Louise.
p. cm.
Includes index.
1. Electric cookery, Slow. 2. One-dish meals. I. Title.
TX827.L695 2008
641.5'884—dc22

2008027158

Printed and bound in the United States of America.
RRD 10 9 8 7 6 5 4 3 2 1

Dedication

For

Betty and Lucile

Joanie and Mikey

Brook and Sam

Acknowledgments

A heartfelt thank you goes out to my editor, Sara Appino, and to those at Sourcebooks who have made this book possible. It takes a special community to build a book and I thank you all.

Contents

Introduction

Welcome to the world of slow, moist cooking. Like most good ideas, the concept of slow cooking has been around for a long, long time. Tried and true, it has simmered and braised meats to fork-tenderness, root vegetables to perfection, and even desserts to savory sweetness.

From the marmite pot to the bean pot, the Chinese clay pot to the colonial Dutch oven, succulent meals have been cooked slowly for centuries. Perhaps the first "slow cooker" was fashioned from an earthen pit lined with heated rocks or smoldering embers, piled high with wild game and gathered vegetables wrapped in moistened corn husks or huge banana leaves. Covered over with a mound of earth, the food cooked, unattended, while people went about their daily tasks of survival. With the advent of the electric slow cooker in the 1970s, slow cooking was raised to a modern art form. Based on ancient concepts (i.e., good food, easily prepared), the slow cooker brought economy, convenience, and flexibility to the modern-day kitchen.

"But that was 1970, and this is the twenty-first century," you say. Well, just think about it for a minute. Wouldn't it be nice to bypass a stop at the deli, the drive-in, the take-out ... and come directly home (your time and budget intact) to a wonderful meal, completed to perfection in your very own kitchen? Just imagine the instant gratification of returning after a long day at work or school, opening the door, and taking in those first comforting aromas of your awaiting meal. With a little advance planning and prep work in the morning, your family can sit down to an economical and nutritious meal in the evening. And won't *you* enjoy it more, knowing clean-up is a breeze when the meal is over!

With the mastery of a few basic concepts and a little creativity, you, too, can enjoy the benefits of slow cooking. This book is meant to provide you with just such ideas and to entice you into the delicious world of family-style, slowly cooked crockery meals.

Getting Started

Slow cookers come in a variety of sizes—from one-quart capacity for singles and small recipes to six-quart capacities for six persons plus and larger-style cooking. To take full advantage of your slow cooker, the recipe should fill the pot at least half- to three-quarters-full for maximum cooking performance. You may find that you will want to have more than one slow cooker, perhaps in varying sizes, to enhance your cooking capacity…a small one for that dip you are serving at a party, a large one for that whole chicken, soup, or stew, and even a medium-size one for a side dish or dessert.

Most commonly, slow cookers have two settings: the "low" setting, which cooks at approximately 200° F and the "high" setting, which cooks at approximately 300° F. The low setting is great for all-day and unattended cooking, allowing for flexibility of timing. It's also great for holding food with little worry about its drying out or scorching your meal—a perfect solution when you are caught in traffic after work or the boss has you stay late to meet a deadline. The high setting is great for Saturday and Sunday meals, when you might want to cut your cooking time in half. Throw in a couple loads of laundry or craft in your scrapbook; go to a movie or sit down and watch a football game; play baseball with the kids or go to the gym; take a quick shopping trip to the mall; or put your feet up and read a good book. Before you know it, your meal is done, and you have been far afield from the kitchen! The general rule is that one hour of slow cooking on high is equal to about 2 to 2½ hours of slow cooking on low. In layman's terms, one hour of cooking time (out of the kitchen) spent at the gym is equal to 2 to 2½ hours of cooking time spent (out of the kitchen) watching a good movie. Sounds good to me! How about you?

There are a few basic safety rules that you should meticulously follow when using your slow cooker. After cooking and serving your meal, the remaining food should *not* be stored in or reheated in the slow cooker. Foods left to cool to below 185° F for any extended period of time are greatly susceptible to bacteria growth. So promptly transfer your leftovers to a container for the fridge and do your reheating in a microwave, on the stove, or in the oven. If you are assembling your dish the night before and storing it in the refrigerator, *do not* mix in any raw meats. Add them in the morning just before you start the cooking process. Any raw marinades should be discarded if not incorporated directly into the cooking process.

Slow cookers are designed for just that, slow and gentle cooking. To avoid cracking, do not subject your crockery liner to extreme and abrupt changes of heat. If you have assembled your dish the night before and are transferring it from the fridge to the heating coils, do not attempt to preheat the base unit to speed up the process. Put the chilled and filled liner into the base unit and turn it on low. It will warm up gently and simmer all day. Likewise, when cleaning your crockery insert, make sure to treat it with the same gentle respect, avoiding abrupt temperature changes. Avoid using abrasive cleaners, as they may scratch the glazed surface of the liner. Spraying your liner with cooking spray before assembling and cooking your dish also makes for quick and easy clean-up. And, obviously, do not submerge the electrical portion in water.

It sounds mundane, but don't forget to turn off and unplug your slow cooker when you're done! A good rule of thumb is to get in the habit of turning off and unplugging it *before* you remove your finished dish to the table. Many a story has been told about removing the liner and leaving the base unit heating away on the counter!

These basics said, be sure to look for more "tips, tricks, and info" interspersed within the text of this book. You'll find serving suggestions, Cook's Notes, and Tips from the Kitchen, which offer information and ideas to guide you along. The recipes for this book have been selected to offer a wide range of versatility from simple to formal, and to please all palates. So let's plug in the pot and get cookin' …

Kathy's Asparagus Potato Soup

Makes 10 servings

- 2 pounds asparagus, trimmed and cut into 1-inch lengths
- 2 large potatoes, peeled and cubed
- 2 medium-sized yellow onions, peeled and cut into slim wedges
- 6 cups chicken broth
- 1 teaspoon salt, or to taste
- ½ teaspoon freshly ground pepper
- ½ teaspoon ground mace
- ¼ teaspoon ground nutmeg
- 3 shakes all-purpose seasoning salt
- 10 tablespoons freshly grated Parmesan cheese

Put all the ingredients, except the Parmesan cheese, in a large slow cooker. Cover with the lid and cook on low all day, or until the vegetables are very tender. Cool the soup, still covered, for 20 minutes or so.

Purée the soup in batches in a blender or in a food processor fitted with a metal chopping blade. Ladle the mixture into heated soup bowls, and top each serving with 1 tablespoon Parmesan cheese.

—from the kitchen of Kathy Gulan

A Tip from the Kitchen...

When garnishing with Parmesan cheese, freshly grated makes all the difference in the world! Parmesan curls are nice, too. Use your potato peeler to shave off curls from the wedge of cheese directly onto the soup.

Farmhouse Chicken and Wild Rice Soup

Makes 8 servings

- 4 chicken thighs, skin removed
- 1 large onion, chopped
- 2 stalks celery, chopped
- ½ cup wild rice, rinsed
- 1 (14.5-ounce can) whole peeled tomatoes with juice (break up tomatoes with wooden spoon)
- 1 (10.5-ounce) can vegetable broth
- 2 tablespoons chicken bouillon granules
- ½ teaspoon dried basil
- ¼ teaspoon dried thyme
- 4 whole garlic cloves
- 1 bay leaf
- 1 (13.25-ounce) can mushroom stems and pieces, drained
- Salt and white pepper, to taste

Combine all the ingredients (except mushrooms) and 6 cups water in the slow cooker. Cover with the lid and cook on low for 8 hours, or until the chicken is very tender and the rice is puffed. Add the mushrooms during the last hour of cooking. Taste the soup and adjust seasonings by adding salt and white pepper. Before serving, remove the chicken from the pot and shred; return the meat to the pot. Remove and discard the bay leaf. Serve.

Cook's Note: For a creamy version of this soup, omit the can of tomatoes. Use chicken breasts rather than thighs. At the end of cooking, stir in 1 to 2 cups half-and-half to suit your taste.

Mom's Chicken Soup

Makes 8 servings

- 1 (3 to 3-plus pounds) whole chicken, rinsed and patted dry; reserve neck and giblets
- 2 onions, chopped
- 2 carrots, sliced
- 2 stalks celery, sliced
- 2 cloves garlic, whole
- ¼ cup chopped parsley
- 4 cups chicken stock
- 1½ teaspoons sea salt
- ½ teaspoon pepper
- ½ teaspoon dried basil
- ½ teaspoon dried thyme
- 1 bay leaf
- 1 cup frozen peas, thawed
- 1 cup frozen corn, thawed
- 1 (7-ounce) can mushroom stems and pieces, drained
- 6 ounces flat noodles

Put all the ingredients, except the peas, corn, mushrooms, and noodles, in the slow cooker. Add 2 cups water. Cover with the lid and cook on low for 8 hours. Remove the chicken from the slow cooker, and cool enough to handle. Remove neck and gizzard and discard; leave the remaining giblets, if desired. Shred the meat, discarding the skin and bones; return the meat to the slow cooker. Turn the slow cooker to high. Add the peas, corn, mushrooms, and noodles; replace the lid and cook until the noodles are tender, about a half hour on high. Adjust seasonings by adding more salt and pepper, if necessary. Remove and discard the bay leaf before serving.

—from the kitchen of Betty Tillman

Cook's Note: If you prefer, cook the noodles according to package instructions in a separate pot and add them to the soup just before serving. Also, you may substitute cooked rice in place of the noodles; add it just before serving.

Aunt Min's Chicken Soup with Matzo Balls

Makes 8 servings

- 1 whole stewing chicken, about 3 to 4 pounds, cleaned and patted dry
- 1 turkey wing
- 2 quarts boiling water
- 2 onions, roughly chopped
- 1 parsnip, roughly chopped
- ½ green pepper, chopped
- 2 stalks celery, sliced
- 4 to 5 carrots, sliced on the diagonal
- 1 to 2 cloves garlic
- 1 tablespoon sugar
- 2 teaspoons salt
- 4 teaspoons jarred chicken-based bouillon paste
- Matzo balls, cooked separately
- Freshly chopped parsley, for garnish

Place the chicken and turkey wing in the slow cooker. Cover with the 2 quarts boiling water. Cover with the lid and cook on high for 1 to 2 hours, quickly skimming off any foam and fats on the surface as needed and returning the lid to the pot.

Add the vegetables and seasonings to the slow cooker. Replace the lid, and cook on low for 4 more hours, or until the chicken and vegetables are tender. Remove the chicken and turkey wing from the slow cooker. Discard the turkey wing. Debone, deskin, and cut up the chicken. Return the meat to the slow cooker; increase the heat to high, and cook, covered, for a half-hour more. At this time, add freshly cooked matzo balls to heat in the soup, if desired. Serve the soup hot, garnished with freshly chopped parsley.

—from the kitchen of June Wallace

June II's Matzo Balls

Makes approximately 8 balls, to be served with Aunt Min's Chicken Soup

This recipe requires advance preparation—make batter and chill overnight.

- 2 tablespoons vegetable oil
- 2 large eggs, slightly beaten
- ½ cup unsalted matzo meal
- 1 teaspoon salt

Blend together the oil and eggs. Mix together the matzo meal and salt; add to the egg mixture. Mix in 2 tablespoons water. Cover and chill the batter overnight.

Bring 2 quarts water to a boil in a large pot. With wet hands, take 1 tablespoon batter at a time and form into balls; don't overwork. Drop gently into boiling water. Repeat until the batter is used up. Cover with the lid and cook for 35 minutes. Don't lift the lid. Don't peek! Remove the matzo balls with a slotted spoon—add to soup or serve with gravy.

Caleb's Broccoli-Potato Soup

Makes 6 to 8 servings

- 3 tablespoons butter
- 1 onion, finely chopped
- 1 large potato, peeled and chopped
- 6 cups canned chicken or vegetable broth
- 3 or 4 cups chopped fresh broccoli, florets and tender stems
- 1 bay leaf
- 1 pint half-and-half, or to taste
- Dash nutmeg
- Salt and white pepper, to taste

Heat the butter in a large skillet over medium heat and sauté the onion to soften. Add the potato and stir to coat. Place the mixture in the slow cooker. Add the chicken broth, chopped broccoli, and bay leaf. Cover with the lid and cook on high until the potato and broccoli are tender, approximately 4 to 6 hours. Remove the bay leaf. Turn the slow cooker to low.

Purée the soup in batches in a blender and return to the slow cooker. Stir in enough half-and-half to reach the desired creamy consistency. Season with salt, white pepper, and nutmeg. Heat on low just until warmed through; do not let the soup boil after adding the cream. Serve immediately.

A Tip from the Kitchen...

Dairy products, such as milk, cream, sour cream, cream cheese, and other cheeses, can curdle and separate if cooked for too long or at too high a temperature. Try to add these during the last hour of cooking or incorporate them on low heat when possible.

Tasty Tortellini Soup

Makes 6 servings

- 1 (14.5-ounce) can diced tomatoes
- 1½ cups chicken broth
- ½ teaspoon dried crushed basil
- ¼ teaspoon pepper
- 2 cups vegetables, such as sliced carrots, frozen thawed broccoli florets, frozen thawed cauliflower, or frozen thawed spinach, squeezed dry
- 1 cup frozen peas
- 1 (7-ounce can) mushroom stems and pieces, undrained
- 8 ounces refrigerated tortellini, as desired
- Freshly snipped parsley, for garnish
- Freshly shaved Parmesan cheese, for garnish

Put the first 4 ingredients in the slow cooker. Add 1½ cups water and the vegetables, except the peas and mushrooms. Cover with the lid and cook on high for 3 to 4 hours. Add the peas, mushrooms, and tortellini. Put the lid back on and cook 1 hour more, until the tortellini is tender. Garnish with the parsley and shaved Parmesan cheese curls and serve.

Cook's Note: Browned crumbled Italian sausage may be added to this soup. Place in the slow cooker at beginning of recipe. Or a vegetarian soup may be made by substituting vegetable broth in place of chicken broth.

A Tip from the Kitchen...

"Gild the lily"—When possible garnish your slow-cooked dishes with a fresh ingredient, such as chopped fresh parsley, snipped fresh chives from the garden, diced sun-dried tomatoes, homemade croutons, a little grated lemon zest, crisped bacon bits, freshly grated cheeses, or cheese curls. The contrast of texture will add surprise and interest to your meal and an extra touch that makes it special.

Creamy Tomato Soup with Cognac

Makes 6 to 8 servings

- 4 tablespoons butter, divided
- 1 onion, chopped
- 15 to 16 garden tomatoes, scalded, skinned, and whole
- 1 teaspoon crushed dried basil
- 1 pint heavy cream
- 1 teaspoon brown sugar
- Salt and white pepper, to taste
- 4 to 5 tablespoons cognac, or to taste

Heat 3 tablespoons butter in a large skillet over medium heat and sauté the onion; transfer the onion to the slow cooker. Partially crush the tomatoes with a fork and add to the slow cooker. Add the basil. Cover with the lid and cook on low for 5 to 7 hours, or until all the tomatoes are stewed and juicy.

Force the tomato mixture through a sieve and discard the pulp and seeds. Put the smoothed mixture back into the slow cooker. Heat the heavy cream with the brown sugar, taking care not to boil it, and stir and whisk it into the tomato-base. Season with salt and white pepper.

In a ladle, flame 4 to 5 tablespoons cognac, and stir it into the soup. Swirl in the remaining 1 tablespoon butter. Serve warm as a first course.

—from the kitchen of Juan Alduncin, as enjoyed on the island of Cozumel

A Tip from the Kitchen...

■ To easily remove the skins from fresh tomatoes, drop the tomatoes into boiling water for 30 seconds, remove with a slotted spoon, and plunge into ice water. The skins will peel off easily. This scalding method works equally well for skinning peaches.

■ For an elegant touch, try seasoning with white pepper in light-colored soups and sauces. Save the black pepper for stews, chilis, and brown sauces.

■ A pat of butter swirled into a soup, sauce, or stew at the very last minute adds depth and hidden flavor to the dish. It's just one little pat! French cooks have used this secret for years, finishing their sauce with a little swirl of butter. Used sparingly, it's a nice addition to your repertoire.

Lentil and Rice Soup

Makes 10 servings

- 2 (16-ounce) cans tomatoes with juice
- 1 (12-ounce) can tomato paste
- 2 cups uncooked lentils
- 2 cups uncooked long-grain rice
- 2 medium-sized onions, chopped
- 2 cloves garlic, minced
- Salt and freshly ground black pepper, to taste

Put the tomatoes with juice and the tomato paste in the slow cooker. Add 8 cups water and stir well. Stir in the remaining ingredients. Cover with the lid and cook on low for 8 to 10 hours, or on high for 4 to 6 hours, until the lentils are soft and the rice is tender. Adjust seasonings, if necessary.

—*excerpted and adapted from* Frozen Assets: Cook for a Day and Eat for a Month *by Deborah Taylor-Hough*

A Tip from the Kitchen...

When chopping onions, Deborah recommends chopping more than you need for your recipe. Package in portioned sizes in freezer bags and store in freezer (for up to 2 months) for future recipes. Next time your recipe calls for chopped onions, they will be ready and waiting ... no muss, no fuss.

Betty's Hearty Lentil Soup

Makes 10 servings

- 2 cups dry lentils, rinsed
- 1 cup chopped carrots
- 1 cup chopped onion
- 1 cup chopped celery
- 2 to 3 cloves garlic, peeled
- 1 to 2 bay leaves
- ½ teaspoon salt
- ½ teaspoon dried marjoram
- ¼ teaspoon white pepper
- 1 (10.5-ounce) can vegetable broth
- 1 meaty ham bone, about 1 pound
- Parmesan-Garlic Toast (recipe follows)

Put the lentils in the slow cooker. Add the remaining ingredients, including 6 cups water, and cover with the lid. Cook on low for 8 to 10 hours. Lift out the ham bone and remove all the meat from the bone. Discard the bone and return the meat to the soup. Adjust the seasonings with additional salt and pepper, if necessary. Remove and discard the bay leaves before serving. Serve with the Parmesan-Garlic Toast on the side.

Parmesan-Garlic Toast

Preheat the oven to broil. Meanwhile, cut 1 French baguette into slices about ½ inch thick. Place the slices on a cookie sheet. Spread them lightly with softened butter. Sprinkle them with some garlic powder and grated Parmesan cheese. Heat the slices under the broiler until toasted and crisped around the edges. Serve with the soup.

—from the kitchen of Betty Tillman

A Tip from the Kitchen...

Soups make a satisfying yet light dinner when accompanied with crusty French bread and a salad. Splurge with a fantastic dessert after this simple meal, and you will be well satisfied. (Check out the dessert section on pages 233–248.)

Split Pea Soup with Ham

Makes 8 servings

- 10 cups water, chicken broth, or mixture of both
- 4 cups dried split peas, rinsed and picked cleaned
- 1 cup diced ham
- 1 cup chopped celery
- 1 cup chopped onion
- 1 cup sliced carrots
- 1 teaspoon salt
- ½ teaspoon pepper
- ¼ teaspoon crushed dried marjoram
- 1 bay leaf

Put all the ingredients into the slow cooker. Cover with the lid and cook on low for 8 to 10 hours. Or cook on high for 6 hours, until the split peas are tender.

—excerpted and adapted from Frozen Assets: Cook for a Day and Eat for a Month, *by Deborah Taylor-Hough*

A Tip from the Kitchen...

What goes better with soup than crackers? It's an automatic! Don't forget those old-fashioned oyster crackers. As a child, I remember plopping those little puffy crackers into my soup. Toss them with a little melted butter and some seasonings and crisp them in a 350 degree oven for about 10 minutes, and you have an excellent garnish for your slowly cooked soup. The oyster crackers may also be crisped, uncovered, using the high setting of your slow cooker, or they may be stirred in a pan. Once cooled, store in an airtight container and use as a snack or garnish.

A Tip from the Kitchen...

Your favorite party mix can be made in the slow cooker as opposed to the oven. Combine assorted cereals, nuts, crackers, and pretzels, along with melted butter and your seasonings of choice, and toast them in an uncovered slow cooker on high for 1 hour. Then, reduce the heat to low for 2 to 4 hours more, stirring every so often. Serve warm straight from the pot! Store cooled in an airtight container.

Aunt Joan's German Bean Soup

Makes 6 to 8 servings

For a different taste and texture, substitute great Northern beans for the kidney beans in this recipe. Serve as a hearty main course with crusty French bread.

- 4 cups canned beef broth
- 2½ cups dried kidney beans, soaked overnight and drained
- 6 slices bacon, finely chopped, sautéed, and drained
- 2 cups diced celery
- 2 cups diced potatoes
- 1 cup diced onion
- 1 cup diced carrots
- ½ cup canned tomato puree
- 2 bay leaves
- 2 cloves garlic, minced
- 1 tablespoon salt
- ¼ teaspoon pepper
- 2 tablespoons red wine vinegar
- 2 cups sliced and fully cooked garlic sausage
- 1 cup thinly sliced leeks or sliced green onions, including tops

Put all the ingredients, except the last three, into the slow cooker. Add 6 cups cold water. Cover with the lid and cook on low for 8 to 10 hours, until the beans are tender and the flavors have melded. Remove and discard the bay leaves. Purée half the mixture in the blender and return it to the slow cooker. Add the vinegar, garlic sausage, and leeks. Continue to heat until warm. The leeks will be crisp-tender.

—from the kitchen of Joan Sennett

Chicken Corn Chowder

Makes 8 servings

- 2 tablespoons butter or margarine
- All-purpose seasoning salt to taste
- 1½ pounds chicken tenders, cut into ½-inch cubes
- 2 small onions, chopped
- 2 celery ribs, sliced
- 2 small carrots, sliced
- 2 cups frozen sweet corn, thawed
- 2 (10.75-ounce) cans cream of potato soup
- 1½ cups chicken broth
- 1 teaspoon dill weed
- ½ to 1 cup half-and-half
- Salt and white pepper, to taste

Melt the butter in a large skillet over medium heat and sprinkle in the all-purpose seasoning. Add the chicken and sauté until lightly browned. Transfer the chicken to the slow cooker. Add the next seven ingredients, cover with the lid, and cook on low for 5 to 6 hours, or until the chicken is done and the vegetables are tender. During the last 15 minutes of cooking, add the half-and-half and adjust seasonings to taste.

—recipe contributed by Michael Gulan

Barbara's "Six-Can" Soup

Makes 6 to 8 servings

- 1 (19-ounce) can minestrone soup with chicken
- 1 (10.5-ounce) can chicken broth
- 1 (14-ounce) can cream-style corn
- 1 (15-ounce) can tomatoes with juice
- 1 (14-ounce) can mixed vegetables, undrained
- 1 (15-ounce) can ranch-style beans

Put all the ingredients in the slow cooker and stir to blend. Cover with the lid and cook on low for 2 to 4 hours, or until thoroughly heated through and the flavors have blended. Serve with crusty French bread; or see Ranch Bread recipe that follows.

Cook's Note: Make it a healthier soup by selecting low-sodium canned vegetables, beans, and soups whenever possible.

—from the kitchen of Rush Hour
reader Barbara

Ranch Bread

Makes 8 to 10 servings

Here is an easy recipe for a delicious bread to accompany your soup.

- 1 loaf French bread, halved down the center lengthwise
- 1 stick butter, softened
- 1 tablespoon dry ranch-style salad dressing mix

Preheat the oven to 350 degrees.

Mix the butter and salad dressing mix to blend. Spread the butter mixture on the two bread halves. Wrap each half in foil.

Bake for about 15 minutes. Cut slices on the diagonal to serve.

Taco Soup

Makes 8 servings

- 2 tablespoons vegetable oil
- 1 to 1½ pounds ground beef
- 1 onion, chopped
- 1 (1.2-ounce) packet taco seasoning mix
- 1 (1- ounce) can dark red kidney beans, drained
- 1 (15-ounce) can pinto beans, drained
- 1 (28-ounce) can stewed whole tomatoes with juice, broken up
- 1 (15-ounce) can Mexican-style diced tomatoes, undrained
- 1 (11-ounce) can whole-kernel corn, undrained
- ¼ cup jarred chili rounds (jalapeno slices)
- 1 to 2 tablespoons juice from the chili rounds jar
- 1 (1.0-ounce) packet ranch-style salad dressing mix
- 1 (8-ounce) block Monterey Jack cheese, cut into eight 1-inch cubes
- 4 or 5 corn tortillas, cut into thin strips and fried, for garnish
- Sour cream, for garnish
- Chili powder, for garnish

Heat the oil in a large skillet over medium heat and brown the ground beef, the onion, and half the taco seasoning. Drain off any excess fat and put the meat mixture in the slow cooker. Add the remaining ingredients and the remaining taco seasoning. Stir to mix. Cover with the lid and cook on low for 6 hours.

To serve, place a cube of cheese in the bottom of each soup bowl. Ladle the soup over the cheese and garnish with crispy tortilla strips, a dollop of sour cream, and a dusting of chili powder.

Cook's Notes: Ground turkey breast meat may be substituted in place of the ground beef. If you prefer a thicker soup, do not drain the cans of beans, but do drain the canned corn.

The Rush-Hour Cook's Chicken Dumpling Soup

with The Rush Hour Cook's Old-Fashioned Dumplings

Makes 6 servings

- 2 tablespoons olive oil
- 1½ pounds chicken breast, cut into pieces
- 4 carrots, chopped
- 2 celery stalks, chopped
- 1 large onion, chopped
- 4 (14.5-ounce) cans chicken broth
- 1 teaspoon garlic powder
- 1 teaspoon salt
- ½ teaspoon pepper
- ½ teaspoon chicken bouillon granules

Heat the oil in a large nonstick skillet over medium heat and brown the chicken pieces. Transfer them to the slow cooker. Add the chopped vegetables, broth, 4 soup cans full water, and seasonings. Cover with the lid and cook on low for 6 to 8 hours, until the chicken is done and the vegetables are tender. Add the dumplings (recipe follows) to the soup. Cover with the lid and increase the heat to high; continue cooking for 30 minutes more, or until the dumplings are shiny and set.

Not-a-Soup, Not-a-Stew Chicken

Makes 6 servings

Serve with French bread for a complete meal.

- 3 tablespoons olive oil
- 2 pounds boneless, skinless chicken breasts, cut into bite-sized pieces
- 1 onion, chopped
- 4 cloves garlic, minced
- 1 cup chopped celery
- 1½ cups frozen mixed vegetables, such as broccoli, cauliflower, and beans, thawed
- 1½ cups frozen carrots, thawed
- 3 cans chicken broth
- 1½ cups frozen peas, thawed
- 1 (8-ounce) package egg noodles, partially cooked
- 1 teaspoon salt
- ¼ teaspoon pepper

Heat the oil in a large skillet over medium heat and sauté the chicken, onion, and garlic for 5 to 8 minutes. Add the celery and cook for 1 to 2 minutes more. Transfer to a slow cooker and add the mixed vegetables, carrots, chicken broth, 1 cup water, salt, and pepper. Cover with the lid and cook on high for 4 to 6 hours, or on low for 8 to 10 hours. During the last hour of cooking, add the egg noodles and the peas, cooking until the noodles are tender and the peas are cooked but not mushy. Adjust seasonings, if desired.

—excerpted and adapted from The Rush Hour Cook Presents Effortless Entertaining *by Brook Noel*

A Tip from the Kitchen...

When adding noodles to your slowly cooked soup, partially cook them beforehand to avoid sticky noodles and a starchy soup.

Patsy's Cabbage Soup

Makes 6 servings

- 1 (26-ounce) can tomato soup
- 1 (12-ounce) can frozen apple juice concentrate, thawed
- 1 head green cabbage, cored and thinly sliced
- 1 onion, sliced
- 1 beef soup bone (optional)

Place all the ingredients in the slow cooker. Cover with the lid and cook on high for 1 hour; turn the setting to low and cook for 4 to 6 hours more. Voila! Soup!

Cook's Note: If using a soup bone, at the end of cooking, remove the bone from the soup. Dice up any usable meat and add it back to the soup.

—from the kitchen of June Wallace

Easy Beef Stew

Makes 6 servings

If your market's produce section does not have already cut-up vegetables, substitute an equal amount of frozen, thawed stew vegetables. Serve the stew with mashed potatoes.

- 16 to 24 ounces mixed stew vegetables, cut up for cooking
- 1½ pounds lean stew beef, cubed
- ½ to 1 teaspoon all-purpose mixed steak seasoning
- 1 (10.75-ounce) can condensed tomato soup
- ½ soup can red wine, broth, or water
- 1 bay leaf
- 1 (7-ounce) can mushrooms, drained

Arrange the stew vegetables in the bottom of the slow cooker. Top with the beef and sprinkle with the seasoning. Mix the soup and wine together, and pour over the ingredients. Add the bay leaf. Cover with the lid and cook on low for 8 to 10 hours. Add the mushrooms during the last hour of cooking. Remove and discard the bay leaf before serving.

Easy Hearty Beef Stew

Makes 6 to 8 servings

- 2 pounds stew beef, trimmed of fat and cut into 1-inch cubes
- 5 carrots, cut into 1-inch cubes
- 1 large onion, cut into chunks
- 3 stalks celery, sliced
- 1 (28-ounce) can tomatoes
- ½ cup quick-cooking tapioca
- 1 to 2 whole cloves or ½ teaspoon ground cloves
- 2 bay leaves
- Salt and freshly ground black pepper, to taste

Put all the ingredients into the slow cooker. Mix thoroughly. Cover with the lid and cook on low for 12 hours, or on high for 5 to 6 hours.

—from the kitchen of Joan Egan

A Tip from the Kitchen...

Raw root vegetables, such as carrots, potatoes, parsnips, and turnips, hold their texture very well during prolonged cooking—in fact, they tend to cook more slowly than the meat. A good rule is to place root vegetables in the bottom of the pot and nestle the meat on top for more even cooking.

Easy Casserole Stew

Makes 6 to 8 servings

- 2 pounds stew beef, trimmed of fat and cut into 1-inch cubes
- 4 to 5 carrots, cut into chunks
- 3 onions, cut into chunks
- 1 cup cubed celery
- 6 potatoes, peeled and halved
- 1 cup chopped green pepper
- 2 tablespoons cornstarch
- 1 tablespoon sugar
- 2 cups tomato juice
- Salt and freshly ground black pepper, to taste

Put the first 6 ingredients in the slow cooker. Mix together the cornstarch and sugar and sprinkle into the slow cooker. Add the tomato juice. Cover with the lid and cook on high for 4 to 6 hours, or until the meat, potatoes, and vegetables are very tender.

—recipe contributed by MaryAnn Koopmann

Bea's Desperation Beef Stew

Makes 6 servings

You may use tomatoes with green chiles, celery, and garlic, but any flavored diced tomatoes will work.

- 1 (3-pound) beef roast
- 1 large zucchini, cut into 1-inch pieces
- ½ pound baby carrots
- ½ pound fresh mushrooms
- 1 (14.5-ounce) can flavored diced tomatoes

Put all ingredients in the slow cooker. Cover with the lid and cook on high for 4 to 6 hours, or until the meat is tender. It's as simple as that.

—from the kitchen of Rush Hour reader Beatriz Newns

June's Three-Step Stew

Makes 6 servings

- 1 (10.75-ounce) can tomato soup, undiluted
- 1 cup water or red wine
- 3 tablespoons all-purpose flour
- 2 pounds beef chuck roast, cut into 1-inch cubes
- 3 carrots, cut into 1-inch diagonal slices
- 6 small white boiling onions
- 4 red potatoes, cut in 1½-inch chunks
- ½ cup sliced celery
- 12 whole mushrooms
- 2 beef bouillon cubes, crushed
- 1 tablespoon mixed Italian herbs
- 1 bay leaf
- Salt and freshly ground black pepper to taste
- Freshly cooked wide noodles

Step 1: Blend together the soup, water or red wine, and flour until smooth; set aside.

Step 2: Put the meat and the remaining ingredients (except salt and pepper) in the slow cooker.

Step 3: Pour in the soup mixture. Cover with the lid, and cook on low for 8 hours, or until the meat is tender. Adjust seasonings if necessary. Serve over wide noodles.

—from the kitchen of June Wallace

A Tip from the Kitchen...

Inexpensive cuts of meats are perfect for slow cooking. Briskets, rump roasts, stew meat, shanks, short ribs, round steak, and chuck roasts are all suitable. These tougher cuts of meat will be fork tender and very flavorful by the end of cooking time, and with less marbling of fat, they will automatically provide leaner results. Take time to trim excess fat off the meat before placing in the slow cooker for even leaner results.

Simply Catalina Stew

Makes 6 servings

Serve this stew with freshly made buttermilk biscuits. For convenience, use refrigerated biscuit dough from the dairy section of your grocery store or a boxed premixed biscuit mix from the bakery section. Bake them up light and fluffy, and have them ready and waiting for the stew.

- 2 tablespoons vegetable oil
- 2 pounds chuck roast, cut into 1-inch cubes
- 1 cup Catalina-style bottled salad dressing
- 8 to 10 new red potatoes, unpeeled
- 1 to 2 cups baby carrots
- 1 teaspoon salt
- ½ teaspoon black pepper
- 1 cup frozen peas, thawed
- Freshly made buttermilk biscuits

Heat the oil in a large skillet over medium heat and sauté the meat; drain. Put the meat in the slow cooker. Add the remaining ingredients, except the peas. Cover with the lid and cook on low for 8 hours, or until the meat is tender. Add the peas during the last half-hour of cooking. To serve, split open the warm biscuits and ladle the stew over top.

A Tip from the Kitchen...

When adding tender vegetables, such as petite peas, zucchini, and fresh mushrooms, do so during the last 15 to 30 minutes of cooking. This will give your vegetables time to add flavor to the dish without dissolving into mush from prolonged cooking. Their crisp-tender quality will add interest and texture to the completed dish.

Fresh Vegetable Medley Stew

Makes 8 servings

This recipe is not meant to be overly seasoned; rather, it is to be served as a subtle and simple dish. Add sides of fluffy, hot brown rice or crusty French bread for sopping up the juices, and you have a hearty and healthy meatless meal.

- 2 medium-sized zucchini, unpeeled and sliced ¾-inch thick
- 2 fresh tomatoes, seeded and cut into chunks
- 2 carrots, sliced ½-inch thick
- 1 small to medium red onion, chopped
- 1 cup sliced celery
- 1 (15-ounce) can garbanzo beans, rinsed and drained
- 1 (15-ounce) can black beans, rinsed and drained
- 3 cups vegetable broth
- 1 (6-ounce) can tomato paste
- 1 teaspoon dried oregano, crushed
- 1 teaspoon dried basil, crushed
- ½ teaspoon sea salt
- ¼ teaspoon black pepper
- ¼ teaspoon red pepper flakes
- 4 cloves garlic, peeled and left whole
- 1 bay leaf
- ½ cup large pitted black olives, cut in half
- Freshly minced parsley, for garnish
- Lime wedges, for squeezing

Put the vegetables in slow cooker, and add the beans. Combine the broth, tomato paste, and dried seasonings, and pour the mixture over the vegetables. Add the garlic and bay leaf. Cover with the lid and cook on low for 6 to 7 hours, or just until the vegetables are fork tender but still hold their shape. , Add the black olives during the last half hour of cooking. Remove and discard the bay leaf before serving. Pass lime wedges to squeeze over the stew.

A Tip from the Kitchen...

Brighten slow-cooked flavors with something fresh at the end of cooking. Garnish your servings with freshly minced parsley, fresh chives, or a squeeze of fresh lemon or lime juice. Or perhaps pass a bottle of special hot sauce, a dollop of salsa or sour cream, or a slice of fresh avocado. Good grated Parmesan cheese, crumbled feta cheese, or sliced buffalo mozzarella also add interest. Crunchy croutons are wonderful, too. Think about the creative ways you can garnish your meals—those little details will make a good recipe great and a simple meal memorable.

June's Family-Favorite Baked Beans

Makes 8 to 10 servings

- ½ pound bacon, cut into 1-inch pieces
- 1 pound ground beef
- 1 large onion, chopped
- 1 (16-ounce) can butter beans, drained
- 1 (16-ounce) can kidney beans, drained
- 1 (31-ounce) can pork and beans, undrained
- ½ cup granulated sugar
- ½ cup packed brown sugar
- ¼ cup ketchup
- ¼ cup barbecue sauce
- 2 teaspoons dry mustard
- 2 teaspoons molasses
- ½ teaspoon chili powder
- ½ teaspoon pepper
- Dash hot sauce, or to taste

Sauté the bacon in a skillet over medium heat until browned; drain on paper toweling. Put the bacon in the slow cooker. Pour off the fat from the skillet and add the beef and onion. Sauté until the beef is browned and the onion is translucent. Drain off the excess fat and add the mixture to the slow cooker. Add the remaining ingredients and stir to mix. Cover with the lid and cook on low for 4 hours to blend flavors. Serve hot.

—from the kitchen of June Wallace

A Tip from the Kitchen...

Baking soda is the cleanser of choice for cleaning a stubborn residue from a crockery liner. Do not use abrasive cleansers that might damage the glazed finish. Let the liner soak with a little baking soda and warm water, and your pot should come clean. Do not attempt to submerge the electrical base unit into water! Clean off with a damp sponge. And always unplug while cleaning!

Sassy Baked Beans

Makes 6 to 8 servings

- 1 pound dried great Northern beans or navy beans, rinsed, drained, and picked clean
- 2 teaspoons baking soda
- 1 onion, diced
- 1½ cups tomato sauce
- ½ cup molasses
- ½ cup dark brown sugar
- 1 teaspoon dry mustard
- 1 teaspoon garlic powder
- 1 shot of Worcestershire sauce
- Salt and freshly ground black pepper, to taste

Bring water to cover to a boil in a large pot. Add the beans and quick-cook for 10 minutes. Remove from the heat and stir in the baking soda. Drain and rinse the beans.

Put the beans in the slow cooker with enough water to cover. Cover with the lid and cook on low heat 10 to 12 hours, or until fork tender. Drain off all but 1 cup cooking liquid. Blend the remaining ingredients (except salt and pepper), mixing well, and stir into the beans. Cover and continue to cook on low for 2 to 4 hours more, until the beans are hot, bubbly, thick, saucy, and cooked to your satisfaction. Adjust seasonings with salt and pepper.

A Tip from the Kitchen...

"No, no, no...Don't peek!" The basic premises of slow-cooker cooking are to surround the contents with hot steam and to maintain a slow, gentle, and even temperature throughout. Remember that every time you lift the lid on your slow cooker, the steam escapes and the cooking temperature drops. It can take up to 15 to 20 minutes for the slow cooker to regain the lost steam and temperature!

Black Bean Chili and Rice

Makes 8 servings

To handle chilies safely, wear rubber gloves while handling them and wash your hands after-wards. Serve this chili over fluffy white rice. Pass lime wedges to squeeze over top of chili.

- 2 (15-ounce) cans black beans, undrained
- 2 (14.5-ounce) cans whole peeled tomatoes with juice, broken up
- 1 large onion, chopped
- 1 green bell pepper, ribbed, seeded, and chopped
- 1 red or orange bell pepper, ribbed, seeded, and chopped
- 1 small chili pepper, ribbed, seeded, and finely diced (wear gloves while handling and wash hands when done)
- 4 cloves garlic, mashed and minced
- 1 to 2 tablespoons chili powder, to taste
- 1 to 2 teaspoons cumin, to taste
- 1 teaspoon crushed oregano
- 1 (15-ounce) can whole-kernel corn, drained
- Lime wedges, for garnish

Put all the ingredients except the corn in the slow cooker. Cover with the lid and cook on low for 5 to 6 hours to blend flavors. Add the corn during the last hour of cooking.

Cook's Note: Spicy chorizo sausage, cut into 1-inch pieces, makes an excellent addition to this recipe—just put it in the slow cooker with everything else and let it spice up the chili.

Grandma's Three-Bean Hot Dish

Makes 8 to 10 servings

- 2 (15-ounce) cans pork and beans
- 2 (15-ounce) cans butter beans, drained
- 2 (15-ounce) cans red kidney beans, drained
- 1 cup brown sugar
- 1 cup granulated sugar
- 1 cup ketchup
- ¼ cup honey
- 1½ pounds bacon, diced and cooked
- 1 pound ground beef, browned
- 1½ cups chopped onion
- Salt and freshly ground black pepper, to taste

Put all the ingredients in the slow cooker, and mix well. Cover with the lid, and cook on low for 3 to 4 hours. Unlike Grandma, go surf the net and come back when it's done.

—recipe contributed by MaryAnn Koopmann, career woman and homemaker

June's Best-Ever Chili

Makes 8 servings

I have this darling neighbor who leaves treats on my doorstep. One of my favorites is her chili—no-frills, simple, but to my taste buds, just perfect. This is a great recipe for those of you who don't like overly thick chili. The baking soda eliminates any sourness in the tomatoes. Serve the chili with soda crackers.

- 2 tablespoons vegetable oil
- 1 pound ground beef, or ½ pound ground beef and ½ pound ground turkey
- 1 small onion, diced
- 1 teaspoon salt
- 1 (28-ounce) can stewed tomatoes, undrained
- 1 (15-ounce) can tomato sauce
- Pinch baking soda
- 1 (16-ounce) can dark red kidney beans, drained
- ¼ cup brown sugar
- 1½ teaspoons chili powder, or to taste
- 1 small green bell pepper, ribbed, seeded, and diced

Heat the oil in a large skillet over medium heat and sauté the meat and onions until browned; season with the salt. Put the mixture in the slow cooker. Add the tomatoes, tomato sauce, and 1 tomato sauce can of water. Stir in the baking soda; the mixture will foam. After 5 minutes, stir in the kidney beans, brown sugar, and chili powder. Cover with the lid and cook on low for 3 to 4 hours. Add the bell pepper during the last hour of cooking. Adjust the seasonings, if needed, before serving.

Cook's Note: This chili freezes well—so don't be afraid to make a big batch.

—from the kitchen of June Kurzon

White Chicken Chili

Makes 6 servings

- 1 (24-ounce) can white beans
- 2 cups cooked and cubed chicken breast
- 1 cup chicken broth
- 2 medium onions, chopped
- 4 cloves garlic, minced
- 2 (4-ounce) cans chopped mild green chilies
- 1 teaspoon ground cumin
- 1½ teaspoons cayenne pepper
- Juice of 1 lime
- Fresh cilantro, chopped coarsely, for garnish

Put all the ingredients, except the lime juice and cilantro, into the slow cooker. Cover with the lid and cook on low for 8 to 10 hours, or on high for 4 to 5 hours. Just before serving, garnish with the lime juice and cilantro.

—excerpted and adapted from Frozen Assets Lite and Easy: Cook for a Day and Eat for a Month *by Deborah Taylor-Hough*

White Chili with Pork

Makes 8 servings

Serve with shredded cheese of your choice and warmed flour tortillas.

- 2 tablespoons vegetable oil
- ½ to 1 pound boneless pork loin, cubed
- 1 large onion, chopped
- 1 (16-ounce) can navy beans, drained
- 1 (16-ounce) can chick peas, drained
- 1 (16-ounce) can white-kernel corn
- 1 (14.5-ounce) can chicken broth or chicken stock
- 1 cup cooked wild rice or mixed-grain rice
- 1 teaspoon ground cumin
- Minced cloves garlic, to taste
- Dash of hot sauce (optional)
- Drained and diced canned chilies, to taste
- Handful of white raisins

Heat the oil in a large skillet over medium heat, and brown the pork and onions until the pork turns light brown and the onions are soft. Transfer the mixture to the slow cooker. Stir in the remaining ingredients. Cover with the lid and cook on low for at least 4 hours to meld flavors, but this can simmer all day.

—from the kitchen of Wendy Louise

A Tip from the Kitchen...

To warm tortillas, wrap them loosely in foil and heat them in the oven, or warm them covered with a paper towel in the microwave. For a real treat, warm them quickly, flipping on each side on a hot griddle. Wrap and bring them to the table in a towel-lined basket complete with a warming stone.

Chili with Chicken and Barley

Makes 6 servings

- 1 tablespoon vegetable oil
- 1 cup chopped onion
- 2 cloves garlic, minced
- 2 cups chicken broth
- ¾ cup quick-cooking barley
- 1 (14.5-ounce) can diced tomatoes with juice
- 1 (15-ounce) can tomato sauce
- ½ to 1 (4-ounce) can chopped green chilies, drained
- 2 teaspoons chili powder
- ½ teaspoon ground cumin
- ½ teaspoon five-spice powder
- ¼ teaspoon ground cayenne pepper
- 1 (11-ounce) can whole-kernel corn, drained
- 3 cups chopped, cooked chicken

Heat the oil in the skillet over medium heat and sauté the onion and garlic for 5 minutes. Put the mixture in the slow cooker. Add the remaining ingredients, except the corn and cooked chicken. Stir in 2 cups water. Cover with the lid, and cook on low for 2 hours. Stir in the corn and the chicken. Replace the lid and cook 45 minutes more.

Cook's Note: For convenience, buy a cooked chicken from the deli and shred the meat.

—from the kitchen of June Wallace

A Tip from the Kitchen...

When adding canned or preserved ingredients to your recipes, go easy on the salt. You may not have to add any! If needed, adjust seasonings to your liking toward the end of cooking time.

CHAPTER 2

Come and Get It! Everyday Entrées

A mainstay of our family's diet, everyday meals make up the majority of our cooking. We all have our favorites and tried-and-trues, but once in a while it's fun to add a new recipe to our collection. So come and get it…we have everything from Chicken in a Pot to Lazy Day Roast in this chapter.

Recipes

- Old-Fashioned Chicken and Rice
  - Chicken–Broccoli Bake Variation
- Sanity-Saving Slow-Cooker Chicken
  - Easy Apple, Nut, and Celery Salad
- Marilyn's Slow-Cooker Chicken and Noodles
- Italian Chicken and Potatoes
- Joan's Chicken in a Pot
- Lemon–Orange Chicken
- Chicken Pattow
- Cranberry Chicken
- Sara's Slow-Cooker Chicken
- Round Steak Casserole
- Rio Roast
- Glenn's Beef and Beer
- Caleb's Favorite Beef Roast
- Braised Beef
- Beef Roast with Onion-Mushroom Gravy
- Marilyn's "Mom's Steak and Gravy"
- Lazy Day Roast
- Easy-Style Homemade Pot Roast
  - German-Style Pot Roast
  - Italian-Style Pot Roast
  - French-Style Pot Roast
- Basic Pot Roast, Plain and Simple
- Simple Swiss Steak
  - Creamy Swiss Steak

- Dad's Beef Brisket
- Miss Kim's Short Ribs and Dumplings in a Pot
  - Dumplings
- L. J.'s Barbecued Ribs
- Judy's Slow Cooker Barbecued Ribs
- Beef BBQs
- Five-Star Sloppy Joes
- BBQ Beef for Sandwiches
- Slow-Cooking BBQ
  - Old-Fashioned Carrot-Raisin Salad
- Hixie's BBQ
- Sara's "Busta Move" Beef Taco Meat
- Slow-Cooker Beef Fajitas
  - Homemade Guacamole-Style Dip
  - Velvety Smooth Avocado Sauce
- Your Choice Pork Chops
- Apple Chops
- Mambone's Pork Chops
- Provençal Pork
- Roast Pork with Vegetables
- Slow-Cooker Pork Chops and Potatoes
- Kielbasa Dinner
- Versatile Sausages and Peppers with Marinara Sauce
  - Meatball Sandwich Variation

Old-Fashioned Chicken and Rice

Makes 6 servings

- 2½ cups chicken broth
- 1½ pounds boneless and skinless chicken breast, cut into 1-inch pieces or strips
- 1½ cups long-grain rice, uncooked
- 1 cup chopped onion
- ¼ cup minced parsley
- 6 cloves garlic, minced
- 1 small red bell pepper, cut into thin strips
- 1 (6-ounce) jar sliced mushrooms, undrained

Combine all the ingredients in the slow cooker. Cover with the lid and cook on high for 3 to 4 hours, or until the chicken is no longer pink and the rice is plumped and tender.

—excerpted and adapted from Frozen Assets Lite and Easy: Cook for a Day and Eat for a Month *by Deborah Taylor-Hough*

Joan's Chicken in a Pot

Makes 6 to 8 servings

- 2 carrots, sliced
- 2 onions, sliced
- 2 celery stalks with leaves, cut into 1-inch pieces
- 1 (3-pound) chicken
- 2 teaspoons salt
- ½ teaspoon black pepper
- ½ cup water, chicken broth, or white wine
- ½ to 1 teaspoon crushed dried basil

Put the vegetables in the bottom of the slow cooker. Season the chicken with salt and pepper and place it atop the vegetables. Pour in the liquid and sprinkle with basil. Cover with the lid and cook on low for 7 to 10 hours, or for 2½ to 3½ hours on high, adding another ½ cup liquid for the longer cooking. Using a spatula, carefully remove the chicken from the slow cooker. Strain the juices and make a gravy if desired.

—from the kitchen of Joan Egan

Lemon–Orange Chicken

Makes 6 servings

- 1 chicken, cut into pieces or left whole
- 2 oranges
- 3 lemons
- Dash dried rosemary
- Dash dried parsley
- Dash paprika
- Salt and freshly ground black pepper to taste
- 6 whole garlic cloves
- ½ cup diced shallots
- ½ cup white wine

Place the chicken in the slow cooker. Squeeze the juice from 2 oranges and 3 lemons over the chicken. Season with the rosemary, parsley, paprika, salt, and pepper. Add the garlic and shallots and pour in the wine. Cover with the lid and cook on low for 6 to 8 hours, until the chicken is falling-off-the-bone tender and the juices run clear.

—from the kitchen of Brook Noel

Chicken Pattow

Makes 6 servings

If you want to shorten the cooking time of this recipe, use thawed peas and chicken instead of frozen.

- 1 box seasoned stuffing mix
- 1 cup frozen peas
- 6 frozen boneless, skinless chicken breasts
- 1 (10.75-ounce) can cream of chicken or cream of mushroom soup
- ⅓ soup can water, white wine, or chicken broth

Place the stuffing mix on the bottom of the slow cooker. Top with peas and chicken breasts. Pour the soup and additional liquid over the top of the chicken. Cover with the lid and cook on low all day.

—from the kitchen of Sara Pattow

Cranberry Chicken

Makes 6 servings

Who says cranberries are just for the holidays—serve up this tasty dish any time of the year! Serve over hot cooked white or brown rice, or for a real treat, serve with freshly cooked wild rice.

- 6 boneless, skinless chicken breast halves
- 1 (1.3-ounce) packet dry onion soup mix
- 1 (16-ounce) can whole berry cranberry sauce
- ½ cup Catalina-style salad dressing

Place the chicken in slow cooker, and sprinkle it with the dry onion soup mix. Mix together the cranberry sauce and salad dressing; pour over the chicken. Cover with the lid, and cook on low for 6 to 8 hours.

Cook's Note: You can substitute any style red French dressing for the Catalina in this recipe.

Sara's Slow-Cooker Chicken

Makes 4 servings

- 1 pound Yukon gold potatoes, quartered
- 4 stalks celery, cut in ½-inch pieces
- ½ large onion, quartered
- 2 tablespoons Italian seasoning, divided
- 1 tablespoon garlic pepper
- 1 tablespoon red wine vinegar
- 4 boneless, skinless chicken breast halves, frozen or thawed*

Place the vegetables in the bottom of the slow cooker. Add 2 cups water, 1 tablespoon Italian seasoning, and the garlic pepper. Place the chicken on top of the vegetables and sprinkle with the remaining 1 tablespoon Italian seasoning and red wine vinegar. Cover with the lid and cook on high for 1 hour; reduce the heat to low and cook for 4 to 6 hours, or cook on low only for 8 hours.

Cook's Note: *If starting with frozen chicken, cooking time may have to be extended another hour.

—from the kitchen of Sara Pattow

Round Steak Casserole

Makes 6 to 8 servings

- 2 pounds round steak, cut ½-inch thick
- Garlic salt, to taste
- Salt and freshly ground black pepper, to taste
- 1 onion, thinly sliced and separated into rings
- 3 to 4 potatoes, peeled and quartered (optional)
- 1 (16-ounce) can French-style green beans, drained
- 1 (16-ounce) can peeled, whole tomatoes
- 1 (10-ounce) can tomato soup

Season the steak lightly with garlic salt, salt, and pepper. Cut into serving-size pieces and put in the slow cooker with onion. Add the potatoes, if using, and green beans. Top with the tomatoes and tomato soup. Cover with the lid and cook on low for 8 hours. Remove the cover during the last half-hour of cooking to reduce the liquid, if necessary.

—from the kitchen of Joan Egan

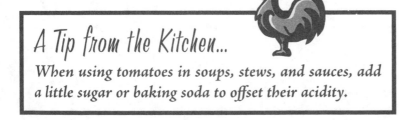

A Tip from the Kitchen...

When using tomatoes in soups, stews, and sauces, add a little sugar or baking soda to offset their acidity.

Rio Roast

Makes 8 servings

- 1 (3- to 4-pound) sirloin tip roast, trimmed of excess fat
- 1 (1.3-ounce) taco seasoning packet
- ½ teaspoon black pepper
- 1 large onion, sliced into thick rings
- 4 carrots, scrubbed and cut into chunks
- 3 potatoes, peeled and quartered
- ½ teaspoon ground cumin
- ½ teaspoon ground coriander
- 1 (10.5-ounce) can beef broth
- 1 teaspoon liquid mesquite smoke

Place the sirloin tip roast in the slow cooker. Sprinkle with the taco seasoning and black pepper. Surround the roast with the onion, carrots, and potatoes. Sprinkle with the cumin and coriander. Combine the beef broth with the liquid smoke and pour over and around the beef. Cover with the lid and cook on low for 8 to 10 hours, until the meat is very tender. Slice and serve with the vegetables and cooking juices.

Glenn's Beef and Beer

Makes 6 servings

Serve over rice, noodles, or mashed potatoes for a hearty no-fuss, no-muss main dish.

- 2 pounds stew beef, trimmed of fat and cut into cubes
- 1 cup all-purpose flour
- 4 tablespoons vegetable oil
- 2 (10.5 ounce) cans beef consommé
- 1 (12 ounce) can beer
- ¼ teaspoon thyme
- ¼ teaspoon oregano
- ¼ teaspoon garlic powder
- ¼ teaspoon onion powder
- 1 bay leaf

Dredge the meat in the flour and set aside. Heat the oil in a large skillet over medium heat and sauté the cubes until golden. Put the meat in the slow cooker, and cover with the consommé, beer, and seasonings. Cover with the lid and cook on low for 8 to 10 hours.

—from the kitchen of Glenn Koopmann

Caleb's Favorite Beef Roast

Makes 8 servings

Serve this dish with freshly cooked noodles and steamed broccoli.

- 1 (3- to 4-pound) sirloin tip beef roast, trimmed of excess fat
- 1 (1.3-ounce) onion soup seasoning packet
- 2 tablespoons vegetable oil
- 2 medium-sized onions, sliced into rings
- 6 cloves garlic, peeled
- 1 (12-ounce) bottle beer
- ½ teaspoon crushed oregano
- 1 teaspoon Worcestershire sauce
- 1 bay leaf
- 2 tablespoons flour
- 1 teaspoon browning and seasoning sauce, or to taste

Season the roast on all sides with the seasoning. Heat the oil in a large skillet over medium heat and brown the roast on all sides. Transfer the roast to the slow cooker. Surround the roast with the onions and garlic. Pour in the beer and add the oregano, Worcestershire sauce, and bay leaf. Cover with the lid and cook on low for 8 to 10 hours. Remove the roast to a warm serving platter and cover with foil.

Meanwhile, increase the heat to high or transfer the cooking liquid to a saucepan on the stove. Remove and discard the bay leaf and remove the garlic cloves. Combine ½ cup water and the flour and whisk until smooth. Add to the juices, stirring and cooking to make a gravy. Add the browning and seasoning sauce to enrich the flavor. Slice and serve the beef with the gravy.

Braised Beef

Makes 6 servings

Serve with a potato dish of your choice and a fresh vegetable or salad.

- 1 tablespoon olive oil
- 2 pounds lean boneless beef, cut into 1-inch cubes, trimmed of excess fat
- 4 cups chopped onion
- 4 cups chopped carrots
- 1 to 2 cloves garlic, minced
- 1 cup dry red wine
- 1 bay leaf
- 1 teaspoon crushed oregano
- 1 teaspoon dried thyme
- Salt and freshly ground black pepper, to taste

Heat the oil in a large skillet over medium heat and sauté the beef and cook the onions until transparent. Transfer to the slow cooker and place the carrots and garlic on top. Pour in the wine and add the seasonings. Cover with the lid and cook on low for at least 6 hours, until the meat is very tender. Add additional wine or water, if necessary. Remove the bay leaf before serving.

—excerpted and adapted from Frozen Assets Lite and Easy: Cook for a Day and Eat for a Month *with Deborah Taylor-Hough*

A Tip from the Kitchen...

The keys to a well-rounded meal are variety and contrast—for example, a complex dish with a simple salad; a spicy dish accompanied with something cool or sweet; a slow-cooked dish along with fresh fruit. Plan your meals to incorporate contrasting textures, colors, and tastes. You will find that many of these recipes offer serving suggestions to help you.

Beef Roast with Onion-Mushroom Gravy

Makes 6 to 8 servings

- 1 (3- to 4-pound) beef roast, trimmed of excess fat
- 1 (1.3-ounce) envelope onion soup mix
- 2 (10.75-ounce) cans cream of mushroom soup
- 1 onion, chopped
- 2 tablespoons steak sauce
- 2 cups sliced fresh mushrooms
- Salt and freshly ground black pepper, to taste

Put the roast in the slow cooker. Combine the soup mix, mushroom soup, one soup can of water, onion, and steak sauce, and pour over the roast. Cover with the lid and cook on high for 7 to 9 hours. Add the sliced mushrooms during the last hour of cooking and adjust the seasonings with salt and pepper, if desired.

—excerpted from The Rush Hour Cook Presents Effortless Entertaining *by Brook Noel*

Marilyn's "Mom's Steak and Gravy"

Makes 6 to 8 servings

Serve over mashed potatoes, noodles, or fluffy cooked rice.

- 2 to 3 pounds round steak, trimmed of excess fat
- 1 (1.3-ounce) envelope onion soup mix
- 4 (10.75-ounce) cans cream of mushroom soup

Cut the meat into 4 x 4-inch pieces and put the pieces in the slow cooker. Pour in the onion soup mix and cover with all 4 cans of soup. Cover with the lid and cook on high for 7 to 8 hours.

—from the kitchen of Rush Hour reader Marilyn Brinkley

Five-Star Sloppy Joes

Makes 6 to 8 servings

- 2 tablespoons vegetable oil
- 1½ pounds ground sirloin
- 1 onion, chopped
- 1 green bell pepper, chopped (optional)
- 1 teaspoon minced garlic
- 2 teaspoons all-purpose steak seasoning
- ½ teaspoon red pepper flakes
- 1 tablespoon red wine vinegar
- 1 tablespoon Worcestershire sauce
- 2 cups canned tomato sauce
- 2 tablespoons tomato paste
- Rolls or hamburger buns, for serving

Heat the oil in a large skillet over medium heat, and when the oil is hot, sauté the meat, onion, green pepper, garlic, and steak seasoning until the meat is browned and the onion and green pepper are limp. Transfer the mixture to the slow cooker. Add the remaining ingredients and stir to mix well. Cover with the lid and cook on low for 2 to 4 hours.

Cook's Note: Serve your Sloppy Joes on tortillas or open-faced on hearty bread slices. For an extra treat, melt Cheddar cheese on top of the open-faced sandwiches. If your family is game, try serving the meat over cornbread! And one last idea—serve over oven-baked French fries and top with melted cheese for a homemade batch of Chili Cheese Fries.

—from the kitchen of The Rush Hour Cook

A Tip from the Kitchen...

This is a good time to remind you to turn off and unplug your base unit before you remove the liner for direct serving at the table.

BBQ Beef for Sandwiches

Makes 12 servings

- 1 (4- to 5-pound) beef chuck roast
- 1 (1.3-ounce) envelope onion soup mix
- 1 (10.75-ounce) can cream of mushroom soup
- 1 cup bottled BBQ sauce
- Kaiser rolls, hoagie buns, or giant hamburger buns, for serving

Put the roast in the slow cooker and sprinkle with the soup mix. Pour in the soup and BBQ sauce. Cover with the lid and cook for 8 to 10 hours on low, or 4 to 5 hours on high. The meat is done when it shreds with a fork. Serve on the rolls.

Slow-Cooking BBQ

Makes 8 servings

- 1 pound small beef cubes
- 1 pound small pork cubes
- 2 cups chopped onion
- 1 cup chopped green pepper
- 1 (6-ounce) can tomato paste
- 1 cup firmly packed brown sugar
- ⅓ cup vinegar
- ½ teaspoon salt
- 2 teaspoons Worcestershire sauce, or to taste
- 1 teaspoon dry mustard
- Hamburger buns, for serving

Combine all the ingredients in the slow cooker. Cover with the lid and cook on low for 12 hours, or on high for 6 hours. Stir and serve on the buns.

Cook's Note: For an extra treat, lightly butter and toast the hamburger buns before filling with the BBQ!

Old-Fashioned Carrot-Raisin Salad

Makes 6 to 8 side servings

Need a good side salad to go with your BBQs? This is a great picnic-style salad to accompany any casual meal.

- 3 cups shredded carrots
- ½ cup diced celery
- ½ cup raisins, or more if desired, plumped in hot water and drained
- ½ to ⅔ cup mayonnaise, or to taste
- Juice from ½ lemon
- Pinch salt

Toss together carrots, celery, and raisins. Mix salad together with not too little but not too much mayonnaise—just enough to bind—and add the freshly squeezed lemon juice. Season with salt and mix again. Cover and refrigerate until serving time.

Cook's Note: Add 1 cup drained, canned pineapple chunks, if desired.

Hixie's BBQ

Makes 6 to 8 servings

- 2 tablespoons vegetable oil
- 1½ pounds ground beef
- 1 onion, chopped
- Salt and freshly ground black pepper, to taste
- 1 cup ketchup
- 2 tablespoons brown sugar
- 2 tablespoons brown mustard
- 3 tablespoons lemon juice
- 1 tablespoon Worcestershire sauce
- ½ cup chopped parsley
- Buns, for serving

Heat the oil in a large skillet over medium heat and sauté the beef and onion. Season with salt and pepper. Drain off any excess fat and crumble the meat. Transfer the mixture to the slow cooker.

Blend together the ketchup, sugar, mustard, ½ cup water, lemon juice, and Worcestershire sauce. Pour the mixture over the meat. Cover with the lid and cook on low for 2 to 4 hours. Add the chopped parsley during the last half hour of cooking. Serve hot on split buns.

—*from the kitchen of June Wallace*

Sara's "Busta Move" Beef Taco Meat

Makes 6 servings

Serve the meat in soft or hard taco shells, on nachos, or in taco salads. You may double the recipe. The addition of hot sauce is Sara's signature ingredient. Use a salsa that is as hot or mild as you like.

- 2 tablespoons vegetable oil
- 1 pound ground beef
- 1 onion, chopped
- ½ cup refried beans
- ¼ cup salsa
- ¼ cup taco sauce
- 1 tablespoon hot sauce
- 1 teaspoon chili powder
- 1 teaspoon pepper
- 1 teaspoon salt

Heat the oil in a large skillet over medium heat and sauté the meat and onion until browned. Drain the fat and put the mixture into the slow cooker. Stir in all the remaining ingredients. Cover with the lid and cook on low for 8 hours.

—from the kitchen of Sara Pattow

A Tip from the Kitchen...

Remember that slow cookers cook optimally when at least half full—on the other hand, not more than three-quarters full. Sometimes you have to customize the pot size to the recipe, or the recipe size to the available pot. This is especially important when cooking for an extended or unattended period of time.

Velvety Smooth Avocado Sauce

Makes about 1 cup

- 1 avocado, peeled and pitted
- 1 tablespoon fresh lemon or lime juice
- Garlic powder to taste
- Sea salt, to taste
- White pepper, to taste

Put the avocado, 2 tablespoons water, lemon juice, garlic powder, salt, and pepper in the blender and process on high until smooth. Pour into a small bowl and cover the surface of dip with plastic wrap—best if made close to serving time.

—from the kitchen of Wendy Louise

Your Choice Pork Chops

Makes 4 to 8 servings, estimate 1 chop per person

Four choices in one simple recipe. Cover with your choice of sauce. How easy is that?

Heat a large skillet over medium heat, and brown the chops well on both sides. Season lightly with salt and pepper and place in the slow cooker.

Cover with one of the following sauces:

- 1 (10.75-ounce) can cream of mushroom soup
- 1 (10.75-ounce) can cream of chicken soup
- 1 (12- to 13-ounce) jar sweet-and-sour sauce
- 1 to 2 cups barbecue sauce

Cover with the lid and cook on low for 6 to 8 hours.

—from the kitchen of Joan Egan

Apple Chops

Makes 4 servings

You may double the recipe for a large slow cooker.

- 1 tablespoon vegetable oil
- 4 pork chops
- 1 cup uncooked rice
- 1 onion, finely chopped
- 1 stalk celery, diced
- 1 teaspoon dried rosemary
- 1 teaspoon dried thyme
- 1 teaspoon salt
- 1 teaspoon pepper
- 2 apples, sliced
- 1 cup water or apple cider

Heat the oil in a large skillet over medium heat and brown the chops on each side for 3 minutes. Set aside.

Put the rice, onion, celery, and seasonings in the slow cooker, mixing well. Top with the apple slices and chops. Pour in water or cider. Cover with the lid and cook on low for 6 to 8 hours.

—from the kitchen of Joan Egan

Mambone's Pork Chops

Makes 6 to 8 servings

Serve with applesauce.

- ½ cup flour
- 1½ teaspoons dry mustard
- 1 teaspoon salt
- ½ teaspoon garlic powder
- 6 to 8 lean pork chops, about 1-inch thick
- 2 tablespoons oil
- 1 (10.75-ounce) can chicken and rice soup

Mix the flour and seasonings in a shallow pan. Dredge the pork chops in the seasoned flour and set aside. Heat the oil in a large skillet over medium heat and brown the chops on both sides. Transfer pork chops to the slow cooker. Add the soup. Cover with the lid and cook on low for 6 to 8 hours, or on high for 3½ hours.

—from the kitchen of Joan Egan

A Tip from the Kitchen...

Pork chops—an often overlooked yet versatile white meat—can usually be bought inexpensively in on-the-bone, family-style packs. On-the-bone chops add extra flavor to the dish. Children love pork—and applesauce on the side offers them a reprieve from tossed salad and the "dreaded vegetable." So serve up some chops and 'sauce for a kid-friendly treat. (See applesauce recipe, page 217.)

Kielbasa Dinner

Makes 6 servings

- ½ head green cabbage, cut into wedges
- 2 large potatoes, peeled and quartered
- 2 to 3 carrots, scrubbed, peeled, and cut into chunks
- 1 onion, quartered and chopped
- 1 teaspoon salt
- ¼ teaspoon white pepper
- ½ teaspoon caraway seeds
- 1½ to 2 pounds smoked kielbasa sausage, cut into 3-inch lengths
- 1 (10.5-ounce) can chicken broth

Arrange cabbage wedges, potatoes, carrots, and onion in the bottom of slow cooker. Sprinkle with salt, pepper, and caraway seeds. Place the sausage pieces on top of the vegetables. Pour the broth over top. Cover with the lid and cook on low for 6 hours.

Cook's Note: If you prefer, you can substitute your favorite bratwurst in place of the kielbasa.

—from the kitchen of Mike Gulan

Versatile Sausages and Peppers with Marinara Sauce

Makes 6 to 8 servings

- 2 tablespoons vegetable oil
- 6 to 8 fresh Italian sausages or bratwurst, cut into 3 to 4 pieces each
- 1 onion, sliced
- 1 (24- to 26-ounce) jar marinara sauce
- 2 to 3 cloves of garlic
- 1 bay leaf
- 1 green bell pepper, ribbed, seeded, and cut into strips
- 1 red bell pepper, ribbed, seeded, and cut into strips
- Freshly cooked pasta or rice for serving

Heat the oil in a large skillet over medium heat and sauté the sausage till browned and the fats are rendered. Using a slotted spoon, remove the pieces to the slow cooker. Sauté the onion for 5 minutes; remove it to the slow cooker. Pour on the sauce. Add the garlic and bay leaf. Cover with the lid and cook on low for 4 to 6 hours. Add the pepper strips during the last hour of cooking. Remove and discard the bay leaf and remove the garlic before serving. Serve over pasta or rice.

A Tip from the Kitchen...

For a Meatball Sandwich Variation: Make your favorite meatballs to replace the sausage pieces in the recipe. Cook as above and serve on hoagie rolls or 6-inch slices of crusty French baguette!

A Tip from the Kitchen...

When using meats, sausages, and the like, take the time to brown them first in a skillet with a little diced onion before adding them to the slow cooker. You can also deglaze the pan to pick up extra bits of flavor, putting those juices in the slow cooker as well. If you prefer not to brown your meats first, add some commercial flavor-enhancing sauce, such as a bottled browning and seasoning sauce. This will enhance and enrich the flavors of the finished dish. You can usually find them in the condiment or specialty-food aisle of your market, and ½ teaspoon or so will greatly enhance your dish.

CHAPTER 3

What's Cookin'?
Hand-Me-Down Entrées

"What's Cookin'?" is a special chapter devoted to inherited recipes from family members and friends. I grew up way before the electric slow cooker was invented and have fond memories of from-scratch recipes simmering on the stove or cooking in the oven. I can still picture my mother standing over the stove, tending to her favorite recipes. The aromas that greeted me when I came home from school were so inviting, and her love and affection, shown to me through cooking, were wonderful gifts.

I think you'll find that you, too, have similar recipes tucked away in your recipe box. I call them "hand-me-downs." With a little experimentation, many of these old standbys can be adapted and formatted for crockery cooking in your slow cooker.

The basic rules to follow are these: replace one hour of conventional cooking with 4 to 6 hours on low, or about 2 to 3½ hours on high. You may need to reduce the liquids in your conventional recipes by as much as half due to moisture retention in the slow-cooking process. You may need to adjust seasonings from conventional recipes for prolonged-cooking satisfaction. So, next time they ask "what's cookin'?," you just might reply with one of your great-grandmother's recipes.

Recipes

Mom's Whole Roasted Chicken

Makes 6 to 8 servings

- 1 lemon, quartered
- 1 small onion, quartered
- 4 cloves garlic
- 1 (3- to 4-pound) whole roasting chicken, rinsed and patted dry, any giblets removed
- 1 to 2 teaspoons olive oil
- 1 teaspoon salt
- 1 teaspoon black pepper
- 1 teaspoon paprika
- 1 teaspoon dried thyme

A Tip from the Kitchen...

You may use any seasonings to ready the chicken for cooking. Try adding chili powder, cayenne, or even curry; garlic salt and lemon pepper; fines herbs or mixed Italian seasoning; or try a commercial seasoning packet of your choice or a mixed poultry seasoning. The sky's the limit, so experiment to find your family's favorite.

Place lemon, onion, and garlic in the cavity of the chicken. Rub the chicken skin lightly with olive oil and season all over with a mixture of salt, pepper, paprika, and thyme. Place the chicken in the slow cooker; add no liquid! Cover with the lid, and cook on low for 6 to 8 hours, until meat is falling-off-the-bone tender and the juices run clear. Remove chicken from the pot, using a spatula for support. Carve or slice the meat, discarding the vegetables.

To make gravy, from the cooking juices, add 2 tablespoons flour moistened with enough water to make a paste; turn the slow cooker to high, or transfer the juices to a saucepan and cook over medium heat until thickened. Adjust the seasoning to your taste with salt, pepper, and ½ teaspoon browning and seasoning sauce.

—from the kitchen of Betty Tillman

Papa Paul's BBQ'd Chicken

Makes 4 to 6 servings

Serve with corn on the cob (see recipe, page 196) and other summer fare.

- 1 (3- to 4-pound) roasting chicken, skinned and cut into serving pieces
- 1 stalk celery, chunked
- 1 small onion, chunked
- ½ cup ketchup
- ¼ cup chicken broth or water
- ¼ cup vinegar
- 1 to 2 tablespoons soy sauce
- 1 tablespoon brown sugar
- 1 teaspoon onion powder
- Salt and freshly ground black pepper, to taste

Place the chicken in the slow cooker with 2 cups water, the celery, and the onion. Cover with the lid and cook on high for 4 to 6 hours, or on low for 6 to 8 hours. Remove the chicken from the slow cooker and set aside. Discard the water, celery, and onion.

Return the chicken to the slow cooker. Make a barbecue sauce by combining the ketchup, broth, vinegar, soy sauce, brown sugar, onion powder, salt, and pepper. Pour the sauce over the chicken, and continue cooking, covered, on low for 2 hours more, or until the chicken is very tender and the sauce glazes the chicken.

—from the kitchen of Paul Tillman, adapted to crockery-style cooking by Wendy Louise

Family-Favorite Garlic Bread

- 1 loaf French baguette
- ¾ to 1 stick butter, softened
- Garlic powder, to taste
- 1 to 2 teaspoons minced chives

Preheat the oven to 350 degrees.

Using a serrated knife, cut the bread on the diagonal into ¾-inch-thick slices, leaving the bottom crust intact. Using a fork, blend together the butter, garlic powder, and chives. Spread the mixture in between each slice, covering the sides of the slices. Wrap the loaf in foil.

Heat in oven for about 15 minutes, until the butter has melted and the bread is heated through. For a crunchy top, unwrap the foil for the last 1 to 2 minutes of heating.

Cook's Note: If the loaf is very long, cut it in half and wrap both halves individually. Serve the first half; turn off the oven to keep second half warm until needed further along in the meal!

—*from the kitchen of Betty Tillman*

A Simple Vinaigrette Dressing for Mixed-Greens Salad

Makes about 1 cup

A simple mixed-greens salad adds depth to any meal.

- 5 tablespoons olive oil
- 2 tablespoons white wine or champagne vinegar
- 1 teaspoon Dijon-style mustard
- 1 tablespoon fines herbs
- ¼ teaspoon garlic salt
- ¼ teaspoon salt
- ¼ teaspoon cracked black pepper
- Pinch sugar

Put all ingredients in a jar, cover with a lid, and shake well to blend. Just before serving, shake the dressing again and lightly dress mixed salad greens of your choice, tossing until the greens are glossy. Refrigerate any leftover salad dressing for another use.

—from the kitchen of Betty Tillman

A Tip from the Kitchen...

When in doubt, we all serve a simple tossed salad at the drop of a hat. Don't forget about the refreshing change of pace that fresh fruit can bring to the table. The addition of mandarin orange slices, grapefruit sections, or fresh pineapple can add interest to your everyday tossed salad. You can also use a sliced fresh peach or kiwi, pairing nicely with your favorite vinaigrette over mixed greens. Be creative and you might get your kids to add salad to their menu.

Lucile's Smoked Pork Chops and Rice

Makes about 1 cup

Serve with a refreshing fruit salad of canned peach or pear halves nestled in lettuce leaves. Top each fruit half with a dollop of cottage cheese, a wedge of cream cheese, or a spoonful of whipped fruit-flavored cream cheese for an instant salad.

- 2½ cups chicken broth
- 1½ cups uncooked long-grain rice
- 1 medium-sized onion, diced
- 1 teaspoon dried parsley flakes
- 1 pinch dried oregano
- 1 (10.75-ounce) can cream of celery soup, undiluted
- Dash Worcestershire sauce
- Minced garlic (optional)
- Freshly ground black pepper, to taste
- 4 boneless, fully cooked smoked pork chops

Mix all the ingredients together except the pork chops, and put half the mixture into the slow cooker. Place the pork chops into the slow cooker, forming a middle layer. Top with the remaining rice mixture. Cover with the lid and cook on high for 3 to 4 hours, until the rice is plumped and tender. Adjust the seasonings, as needed.

—*from the kitchen of Lucile Feiereisen, adapted for crockery-style cooking by Wendy Louise*

Mom's Pork Chops with Scalloped Potatoes

This dish smells divine while cooking.

- 1 bone-in pork chop per person
- Salt and freshly ground black pepper, to taste
- Flour
- Butter
- Milk
- Crushed dried oregano to taste

Thinly slice the potatoes and place them in the slow cooker, seasoning with salt and pepper as you go. Sprinkle a little flour over the potatoes and dot with butter. Arrange the pork chops on top of the potatoes. Pour enough milk over the chops and potatoes to cover halfway. Sprinkle with oregano. Cover with the lid and cook on low for at least 6 hours, or until the pork chops are thoroughly cooked and the potatoes are fork tender. If cooked on high, you can reduce the cooking time to about 4 hours.

—from the kitchen of Betty Tillman, adapted for crockery-style cooking by Wendy Louise

A Tip from the Kitchen...

You will notice in these hand-me-down recipes that measurements and precision fall by the wayside. A casualness takes over as the recipes become more descriptive than directive. We are talking in grandmother, mother, and mother-in-law language now. They measured with a hollow palm, a dollop, a dab, a pat, a package, a peck, a lug, and a pinch for good measure.

Mom's Stuffed Flank Steak

Makes 4 to 6 servings

You can make your own breadcrumbs with about 4 slices of day-old bread cut into cubes, sprinkled with the seasonings of your choice, and sautéed in a little butter and minced onion for flavor.

- 1 very large flank steak
- 8 ounces packaged seasoned stuffing-style bread cubes
- 2 tablespoons vegetable oil
- ½ cup broth or water

A Tip from the Kitchen...

For a spicier version of this same recipe, marinate the scored steak in Italian- or Russian-style salad dressing before stuffing. Remove the steak from the marinade and discard excess marinade; stuff the steak and proceed per recipe instructions.

Score the flank steak with a sharp knife, making a diagonal pattern of slashes across the grain. Put the stuffing down the center of the steak, and roll it up jelly-roll fashion, with the scored side facing out. Secure the roll with toothpicks.

Heat the oil in a large skillet over medium heat and brown the steak on all sides. Spray the slow cooker with nonstick cooking spray. Transfer the meat to the slow cooker and add the broth. Cover with the lid and cook on low for 6 to 9 hours, or on high for 3½ to 5 hours. During cooking, add small amounts of additional broth if needed. To serve, remove the toothpicks and cut into ½-inch thick serving slices, exposing the filling. Arrange the slices on a platter and drizzle with the cooking juices.

—from the kitchen of Betty Tillman, adapted for crockery-style cooking by Wendy Louise

Caleb's Brats 'N Beer

- 2 bratwurst sausages per person
- Buns or rolls
- Beer
- Whole peppercorns, to taste
- Red pepper flakes, to taste

Variation 1

Pierce the sausages with a fork and place them in the slow cooker. Pour on enough beer to cover. Add the seasonings, cover with the lid, and precook the sausages on high for about 4 hours or until plumped, juicy, and fully cooked. Timing isn't really critical. Go off to water ski or play your guitar. When you return, finish the sausages on the grill, browning them nicely. Serve them on buns or rolls with corn on the cob (page 196).

Variation 2

If it's raining and you can't go skiing, pierce the sausages with a fork, and brown on all sides in a skillet. Place in slow cooker with the beer and seasonings and finish cooking. Hold on low setting until ready to serve. Gather a bunch of friends and watch ski videos until you are ready to eat.

—*recipe submitted by Rob Bensen*

A Tip from the Kitchen...

Take advantage of cooking with a slow cooker in the summertime—it takes both the heat and the cook out of the kitchen!

Julie's "Ring-the-Dinner-Bell" Bell Peppers

Makes 8 servings

- 8 large bell peppers, green, yellow or red
- 3 tablespoons vegetable oil
- 1 to 1½ pounds ground beef
- 1 onion, diced
- 2 large tomatoes, diced
- 2 tablespoons vinegar
- 1 teaspoon sugar
- 1 teaspoon ground cinnamon
- ¼ teaspoon ground cumin
- 1 teaspoon sea salt
- ½ cup raisins, plumped and drained
- Green chilies or chili powder, to taste
- ½ cup slivered almonds or pine nuts (optional)

Cap the peppers and remove the ribs and seeds. Set aside.

Heat the oil in a large skillet over medium heat and cook the beef and onion until the onion is transparent and the meat is browned. Drain off any excess fat. Add the rest of the ingredients (except the nuts) and mix well. Gently pack the filling into the peppers. Spray the slow cooker with nonstick cooking spray. Carefully place the peppers, side by side, into the slow cooker. Pile any extra filling on top of all, if necessary. Cover with the lid and cook on low for 4 to 6 hours, until the peppers are tender but still hold their shape and the filling is set. Garnish with slivered almonds or pine nuts, if using.

—*recipe submitted by Wendy Louise*

Mary's Special Meatballs

Makes 8 to 10 servings, allow 2 large meatballs per serving

Serve meatballs with sauce over buttered noodles or with mashed potatoes on the side.

Meatballs

- 1 pound onions, sliced into rings
- 4 pounds ground beef
- Minced onion, to taste
- Minced garlic, to taste
- Salt and freshly ground black pepper, to taste
- 2 cups crushed cornflakes
- 1 cup apple sauce
- 2 eggs, beaten
- 3 to 4 tablespoons vegetable oil

Combine the ingredients, except the oil, and form into large meatballs. Heat the oil in a large skillet over medium heat and brown all the meatballs. Transfer the meatballs to the slow cooker.

Sauce

- 4 tablespoons butter
- ⅓ cup all-purpose flour
- 1 medium-sized onion, diced
- 4 cups beef broth
- 1 (12-ounce) bottle chili sauce
- ⅓ cup tomato paste
- Garlic, to taste
- Crushed basil, to taste
- Freshly ground black pepper, to taste
- 2 tablespoons beef concentrate
- 1 tablespoon Worcestershire sauce
- ½ cup red wine or water
- 1 (8-ounce box) sliced fresh mushrooms
- Butter, for sautéing

Melt the butter in a large saucepan over medium heat, and when it is melted and bubbly, stir in the flour to make a roux. Add the remaining ingredients, except the mushrooms, and cook, stirring constantly, until the mixture thickens. Pour the sauce over the meatballs already in the slow cooker. Cover with the lid and cook on low for 6 to 8 hours, or on high for 3 to 5 hours. Sauté the fresh mushrooms in a little butter, and add to the slow cooker during the last half-hour of cooking.

—from the kitchen of Mary Propernick, adapted for crockery-style cooking by Wendy Louise

A Tip from the Kitchen...

To stay organized, read through your complete recipe, start to finish, before you start cooking. Make sure you understand all the steps involved and have all your ingredients on hand before you begin—and cooking will be a breeze.

Val's Favorite Meatloaf

Makes 6 to 8 servings

Nothing says comfort food like a good meatloaf. Add a favorite vegetable and a side of mashed potatoes, and dinner is served. Make meatloaf sandwiches the next day with leftovers.

- 1 large onion, cut into rings, plus 1 medium-sized onion, finely chopped
- 2 to 2½ pounds lean ground beef
- 1 cup crushed saltine-style crackers or 1 cup cubed day-old bread
- ½ cup ketchup or chili sauce
- 2 teaspoons prepared horseradish
- 1 teaspoon Worcestershire sauce
- 1 teaspoon salt
- ½ teaspoon pepper
- ½ teaspoon crushed dried oregano
- ¼ teaspoon garlic powder
- 1 large egg
- 3 or 4 slices Cheddar cheese

Place the onion rings in the bottom of the slow cooker. Mix the ground beef gently with the remaining ingredients, except for the Cheddar cheese, and form the mixture into a loaf; do not overwork. Place the loaf on the bed of onion rings. Cover with the lid and cook on low for 6 to 8 hours, until the loaf is cooked through. Cover the top of the meatloaf with Cheddar cheese slices during the last few minutes of cooking. Continue to cook until the cheese is just melted. Lift the loaf out of the slow cooker with a spatula; discard the onion rings and juices in the bottom of the pot. Slice to serve.

Cook's Note: Add a cold and refreshing salad to complete the meal (see Frozen Apple Salad recipe on next page).

Auntie Joan's Frozen Apple Salad

A cold and refreshing salad to serve with your slow-cooked meals.

- 1 (9-ounce) can crushed pineapple, drained, liquid reserved
- 2 eggs, slightly beaten
- ½ cup sugar
- Dash salt
- 3 tablespoons lemon juice
- 2 cups peeled, finely chopped apple
- ½ cup finely chopped celery
- 1 cup whipping cream, whipped stiff
- Lettuce leaves, for serving

Measure the pineapple liquid, adding water, if necessary, to make ½ cup liquid. Combine the eggs, sugar, salt, lemon juice, and the reserved liquid. Cook over low heat, stirring until somewhat thickened. Chill.

Stir the pineapple, apples, and celery into the chilled mixture. Fold in the stiffly whipped cream. Pour the mixture into an 8- or 9-inch square freezer-safe dish. Cover and place in the freezer. To serve, cut the frozen salad into squares, and place each serving on a lettuce leaf.

Cook's Note: The frozen salad may be cut about 40 minutes in advance and placed in the refrigerator. Or cut 20 minutes ahead and place it on the table.

Betty's Lamb with Burgundy Sauce

Makes 6 servings

Serve with mashed potatoes and/or crusty French bread.

- 2 tablespoons vegetable oil
- 6 shoulder-cut lamb chops
- 1 large onion, sliced into rings
- 4 or 5 carrots, cut into chunks
- 1 cup Burgundy wine
- 1 (10.5-ounce) can beef broth or beef bouillon
- Flour, for thickening
- Salt and freshly ground black pepper, to taste

Heat the oil in a large skillet over medium heat and brown the chops on each side. Add the onion rings and let them glaze in the pan juices. Transfer the chops and onions to the slow cooker. Add enough water just to cover the chops. Add the carrots and Burgundy. Cover with the lid and cook on low for 6 to 8 hours. Add beef broth and continue cooking for another hour, until the chops are fork tender.

Increase the heat to high. In a separate dish, blend together about 2 tablespoons flour and about ¼ cup water to make a smooth thickening agent. Slowly blend the mixture into the slow cooker juices to thicken the gravy, stirring until incorporated. Cook, uncovered, until the gravy thickens to your liking. Adjust seasonings.

—from the kitchen of Betty Tillman, adapted for crockery-style cooking by Wendy Louise

A Tip from the Kitchen...

Cooking with wine, whisky, sherry, and beer can add special flavor to your recipe and help tenderize the meat. You may replace any of these with an equal amount of water, broth, tea, or fruit juice, if you prefer.

Mother's Garden Stew with Dumplings, Spatzen, or Spaetzle

Makes 6 servings

This is served with dumplings, spatzen or spaetzle; the recipes follow.

- 2 to 3 tablespoons vegetable oil
- Round steak, cut into 6 generous ½-inch thick slices
- Flour
- Butter
- Salt and pepper
- Oregano, crushed between fingers
- Garlic powder
- Fresh green beans (preferably picked from the garden), cleaned and deveined, ends and tips snipped off
- Cooking sherry or port (optional)

In skillet, brown round steak slices (dusted with flour) in a little butter. While browning, season the meat with salt, pepper, oregano, and garlic powder, to taste. Transfer the slices to a slow cooker and add 1 cup water. Cover. Cook on high heat setting until meat is very tender (approximately 2 to 4 hours), adding more water if necessary.

During the last half-hour of cooking add 6 handfuls of freshly picked and cleaned green beans. Add a dash of cooking sherry or port to taste (optional). Return cover to slow cooker and continue to cook on high setting until beans are tender, crisp, and chewy. During last 15 minutes of cooking, add Mother's Old-Fashioned Dumplings. Cover with the lid and continue to cook on high until the dumplings are shiny and firm.

A Tip from the Kitchen...

Many of these heirloom recipes do not have exact measurements. As I mentioned before, our mothers used to cook with a little bit of this and a little bit of that. If something wasn't available, they just substituted something else. Somehow, their meals always turned out creatively delicious; and if we cleaned our plates we were rewarded with a fabulous dessert. So clean up your plate! And check out the desserts chapter on pages 223 through 248.

Mother's Old-Fashioned Dumplings

Makes 8 servings; recipe may easily be halved

- 2 cups all-purpose flour
- 4 teaspoons baking powder
- ½ teaspoon salt
- 1 pinch dried oregano
- 1 cup whole milk

Mix all into a blended batter, taking care to not overmix! Drop by teaspoonfuls onto the cooking stew. Cover and continue cooking on high. Cook until the dumplings are shiny and firm. The dumplings will automatically thicken the stew, forming a nice gravy.

Or, you can cook your dumplings separately in a pot of boiling water. They will automatically float to the top when done. This takes about 10 to 15 minutes. They make a delicious addition to soups and other stews found in this book, or simply served as a side dish, drizzled with melted butter.

—from the kitchen of Lucile Feiereisen, adapted for crockery-style cooking by Wendy Louise

A Tip from the Kitchen...

When cooking dumplings in a slow cooker, take care to make them small, dropping them by teaspoonfuls, rather than tablespoonfuls, for quicker and more even cooking.

Lucile's Spatzen

Makes 4 servings

- 1 egg, well beaten
- ½ teaspoon salt
- ⅓ cup water
- ¾ cup all-purpose flour
- Melted butter to taste

Mix all ingredients, except melted butter, together to form a smooth, soft dough. Drop by small teaspoonfuls into a pot of boiling water. Cover, and cook about 10 minutes. Drain in a colander, and toss with melted butter. Serve these mini dumplings as a side dish for stews and meat-with-gravy dishes in place of potatoes.

Lucile's Spaetzle

Makes 4 servings

Fold 1 tablespoon oil into the previous recipe's dough and blend until smooth. Force the dough through the holes of a colander into the boiling liquid, or form the dough into a patty shape on waxed paper or an oiled surface, slice off noodle-shaped slivers, and slide them into boiling liquid. These mini-noodles only need about 5 minutes to cook. Toss with melted butter and serve as above.

—*from the kitchen of Lucile Feiereisen*

Hunter's Delight

Makes 6 servings

- 2 tablespoons vegetable oil
- 2½ pounds ground beef
- 1 large onion, chopped
- 6 large potatoes, sliced
- 2 (15-ounce) cans whole kernel corn, drained
- 1 (7-ounce) can mushrooms, drained
- 1 diced green pepper
- 1 (10.75-ounce) can cream of mushroom soup
- 1 soup can full whole milk
- Salt and freshly ground black pepper to taste

Heat the oil in a large skillet over medium heat, and cook the ground beef until it is almost browned; drain it, and put it into the slow cooker. Add the onion, potatoes, corn, mushrooms, and green pepper to the slow cooker. Mix in the soup and milk, stirring to blend. Cover with the lid, and cook on low for 3 hours, or until potatoes are tender.

—from the kitchen of Glenn Koopmann

Tuscan-Style Pork Roast

Makes 8 to 12 servings

- 1 (3- to 4-pound) boneless pork roast
- 4 cloves garlic, slivered
- 2 tablespoons olive oil
- 1 tablespoon rosemary
- ½ teaspoon salt
- ½ teaspoon black pepper
- ½ cup dry white wine

Make small slits in the roast and insert the garlic slivers. In a small bowl, mix the oil, rosemary, pepper, and salt. Rub the roast with the seasoning mixture and place in the slow cooker. Pour ½ cup wine over the roast. Cover with the lid and cook on low for 8 to 10 hours, until the meat is incredibly tender.

—*excerpted and adapted from* The Rush Hour Cook: Weekly Wonders *by Brook Noel*

A Tip from the Kitchen...

Try cutting slits in the meat and inserting the peeled garlic directly into the roast for added flavor.

Mom's Easy as 1-2-3 Pork Roast

Makes 4 to 6 servings

Serve this with mashed potatoes.

- 1 (2- to 3-pound) pork loin
- 1 (1.3-ounce) envelope dry onion soup mix

Rub the meat with the soup mix and put it in the slow cooker. Add ½ cup water. Cover with the lid and cook on low for 8 to 10 hours. Make gravy from the roasting juices, if desired.

—recipe submitted by Craig Heun

Mom's Marinated Pork Roast

Makes 4 to 6 servings

If you can, marinate the meat overnight to blend the flavors.

- ¼ cup soy sauce
- ¼ cup dry sherry
- 2 cloves garlic, minced
- 1 tablespoon dry mustard
- ½ teaspoon ground ginger
- ½ teaspoon dried thyme
- 1 (2- to 3-pound) pork roast

Put the roast in a large container and set aside. Make a marinade with the soy sauce, sherry, garlic, mustard, ginger, and thyme, and pour the mixture over the roast. Cover the container and refrigerate the meat overnight.

To cook, place the roast and the marinade in the slow cooker and add ½ cup water. Cover with the lid and cook on low for 8 hours, until the meat is very tender. Serve with your favorite side dishes.

Cook's Note: Looking for a quick and versatile fruit salad to serve with dinner? This is it. See the following recipe.

—from the kitchen of Betty Tillman

Fresh Fruit Salad with Yogurt-Honey Dressing

Makes 1 cup

Choose your favorite fruits and mix with this sweet yogurt dressing for a refreshing salad.

- ¾ cup plain or vanilla low-fat yogurt
- 1 to 2 tablespoons fresh lime juice
- ¼ cup honey
- 1 tablespoon confectioners' sugar (optional, for a sweeter dressing)
- Fresh fruits of your choice, sliced or cut into bite-sized pieces

Mix the yogurt, lime juice, and honey till blended and smooth. Add the confectioners' sugar, as desired, if you wish. Cut all the fruit into bite-sized pieces. Refrigerate the fruit and dressing separately. Toss the fruit with the dressing just before serving.

Mikey's Stuffed Cabbage Rolls

Makes 6 servings (2 rolls per person)

- 12 large green cabbage leaves, tough core removed
- 1 pound ground beef
- 1 cup cooked white or brown rice
- ¼ cup finely chopped onion
- ¼ cup breadcrumbs
- 1 egg, beaten
- 2 tablespoons golden raisins (optional)
- ½ teaspoon all-purpose seasoning salt
- ¼ teaspoon ground cumin
- 1 (15-ounce) can tomato sauce
- 1 tablespoon lemon juice
- 1 to 2 tablespoons brown sugar
- 1 bay leaf
- Fluffy cooked rice, for serving

Bring a large pot of water to the boil and remove from heat. Soften the cabbage leaves in the hot water until limp, about 5 minutes. Drain and set aside to cool.

Meanwhile, in a bowl, make the filling: mix together the beef, rice, onion, breadcrumbs, egg, raisins (if using), seasoning salt, and cumin. Mound one-twelfth of the filling in the center of each cabbage leaf, and roll up envelope-style, folding in the ends to completely encase the filling. Secure the rolls with toothpicks.

Spray the slow cooker with nonstick cooking spray. Lay the rolls in the slow cooker, seam side down, stacking as needed. Mix together the tomato sauce, lemon juice, and sugar; pour the mixture over the rolls. Add the bay leaf to the pot. Cover with the lid and cook on low for 6 to 8 hours. Remove and discard the bay leaf before serving. Serve the rolls on a bed of fluffy cooked rice.

Lamb Variation

As a variation, you may substitute ground lamb in place of the ground beef. Replace the can of tomato sauce with 1 (10.75 ounce) can of beef broth and 1 (14.5 ounce) can of whole peeled tomatoes, broken up and drained. Proceed with recipe as written.

—from the kitchen of Mike Gulan

Sara's Lovely Little Links Casserole

Makes 8 servings

- 1 onion, chopped
- 8 potatoes, sliced
- 2 (16-ounce) packages mini-smoked sausage links
- 1 (16-ounce) bag frozen peas, unthawed
- 1 (10.75-ounce) can cream of mushroom soup
- 1 (10.75-ounce) can cream of celery soup

Place ingredients, in this order, in the slow cooker: onion, potatoes, sausages, peas, and both soups. Cover with the lid and cook on low for 6 to 8 hours.

—from the kitchen of Sara Pattow

CHAPTER 4

Dinner Is Served: Fancier Entrées

Bring out the china, press the napkins, and light the candles. These recipes are for special dinners when you want to entertain with creativity and flair. Or maybe you are having a formal family night with an un-hurried dinner and catch-up conversation. We all appreciate a change of pace now and then, and a relaxed dinner with fancier fare just might be the answer.

Recipes

- Bacon-Wrapped Chicken Breasts
- Bacon-Wrapped Chicken Breasts #2
- Slow-Cooking Chicken Cacciatore
- Mediterranean Chicken with Olives and Capers
- Company's Coming to Dinner Chicken
- Chicken Parisian
- Chicken with Champagne and Cream
- Two Perfect Pork Roasts:
  - The Bachelor's Perfect Pork Roast
  - Pork Roast Perfection
  - Venison Variation
- Beef in Wine Sauce
- Brook's Beef Burgundy
- Dorothea's French-Style Meat Loaf
- Rouladen (German Beef Rolls)

- Slow-Cooker Chinese Beef with Broccoli and Rice
- Pepper Steak
- 4-Way Rock Cornish Game Hens
- Game Hens Mexicana
- Change of Pace Salsa
- Venison Braised with Root Vegetables and Wine
- Easy Venison Roast
- Poached Wild Salmon
  - Easy Hollandaise Sauce
  - Dill Sauce
  - Dill-Chive Butter
- Dad's Pheasant or Partridge Dinner

Bacon-Wrapped Chicken Breasts

Makes 4 servings

Serve on buns, with crusty bread and a broccoli side dish, or with your favorite potato dish.

- 4 boneless, skinless chicken breast halves
- 8 slices thick-cut smoked bacon
- 1 (16-ounce) bottle favorite BBQ sauce
- 1 shot whiskey, preferably Jack Daniels
- 1 tablespoon hot sauce

Wrap the chicken breasts with 2 bacon strips each and set aside. Pour BBQ sauce, whiskey, and hot sauce into slow cooker. Place wrapped chicken breasts in pot and cover with the lid. Cook on low for 6 to 8 hours.

—from the kitchen of "Miz Malibu"

Mediterranean Chicken with Olives and Capers

Makes 4 servings: 1 quarter chicken per person

- About 2 tablespoons olive oil
- 1 whole chicken, cut into quarters, with or without skin
- 1 (15-ounce) can whole peeled tomatoes, undrained and broken up
- ¼ cup red wine or chicken broth
- 2 tablespoons brown sugar
- 2 tablespoons red wine vinegar
- 2 tablespoons tomato paste
- 2 teaspoons dried oregano
- 1 teaspoon dried basil
- 1 cup whole Mediterranean-mixed olives or large green olives
- 4 garlic cloves, whole
- 1 bay leaf
- 1 (7-ounce) can mushrooms, drained
- Hot cooked brown rice for serving
- 2 tablespoons capers, drained, for garnish

Heat the olive oil in a skillet over medium heat and brown the chicken pieces; place them in the slow cooker. Mix together the tomatoes, wine, sugar, vinegar, tomato paste, oregano, and basil. Pour the mixture over the chicken. Add the olives, garlic, and bay leaf. Cover with the lid and cook on low for 7 to 8 hours. Fold in the mushrooms during the last half-hour of cooking. When ready to serve, remove and discard the bay leaf. Serve with freshly cooked rice and garnish each portion with a sprinkling of capers.

—from the kitchen of Wendy Louise

A Tip from the Kitchen...

Check out the salad bar at your market and buy just the amount of specialty olives you need. Use pitted olives, if possible.

Company's Coming to Dinner Chicken

Makes 6 to 8 servings

Add a loaf of crusty French bread and a nice salad, and you have it made!

- 1 medium-sized onion, coarsely chopped
- 4 cloves garlic, peeled and crushed
- 8 to 10 baby new potatoes, scrubbed and peeled around their centers only
- 2 carrots, cut into chunks
- 2 stalks celery, cut into chunks
- 1 (3- to 4-pound) whole chicken
- 1 to 1½ tablespoons butter
- 1 lemon, halved or quartered
- ¼ cup vermouth
- ¼ cup chicken broth
- Salt and freshly ground black pepper, to taste
- Paprika (optional)

Arrange the onion, garlic, potatoes, carrots, and celery in the bottom of the slow cooker. Nestle the whole chicken, breast-side up, into the vegetables. Dot the cavity with butter. Squeeze the lemon juice over all. Immerse the rinds down into the vegetables. Drizzle the vermouth and chicken broth over all and add salt and pepper. Sprinkle the chicken with a dusting of paprika for color, if desired. Cover with the lid and cook on low for 8 to 10 hours, until the chicken is literally falling from the bone.

To serve, carefully remove the whole chicken to a deep platter and surround it with a border of the cooked vegetables and their juices, discarding the lemon rinds.

—originally cooked in a clay pot, adapted for slow cooker-style cooking from the kitchen of Wendy Louise

Chicken Parisian

Makes 6 servings

- 6 medium-sized chicken breasts
- Salt and freshly ground black pepper, to taste
- Paprika to taste
- ½ cup dry white wine, vermouth, or broth
- 1 (10.5-ounce) can condensed cream of mushroom soup
- 1 (4-ounce) can sliced mushrooms, drained
- 1 cup sour cream, mixed with ¼ cup flour

Sprinkle chicken breasts lightly with salt, pepper, and paprika. Put the chicken into the slow cooker. Mix together the white wine, soup, mushrooms, and the flour-thickened sour cream. Pour the mixture over the chicken breasts. Sprinkle with additional paprika. Cover with the lid and cook on low for 6 to 8 hours. Serve the chicken and sauce over rice or noodles.

—from the kitchen of Joan Egan

A Tip from the Kitchen...

Get out the linen napkins. Have your kids set the table and fold the napkins into fancy folds and place in the center of each plate. (There are even books on napkin folding!) Or flare the napkins out of long-stemmed glasses. Put a pitcher of ice water, flavored with lemon slices, on the table. Kids love to drink out of special glasses, and you'll add to your daily water quotient as well!

Chicken with Champagne and Cream

Makes 6 servings

Garnish each serving with a large slice of sautéed portobello mushroom and sprigs of fresh chive for that extra touch.

- 6 boneless, skinless chicken breast halves
- 1 teaspoon dried thyme, crushed
- Salt and white pepper, to taste
- 1 stick plus 1 tablespoon butter
- 1 tablespoon all-purpose flour
- 1 cup champagne
- 1 ½ cups heavy cream
- Portobello mushroom slices, for garnish (optional)
- Chive sprigs, for garnish (optional)

Season the chicken breasts with thyme, salt, and pepper. Heat the 1 stick butter in a large skillet over medium heat and sauté the breasts until just golden. Transfer the chicken to the slow cooker. In the skillet, add the flour, stirring to make a roux. Stir in the champagne and cook until the sauce thickens. Pour the sauce over the chicken. Cover with the lid and cook on high for 3 to 4 hours, until the chicken is very tender. Remove the chicken from the slow cooker, and keep warm on a heated platter. Reduce the heat to low and stir in the heavy cream. Cook only until the sauce is heated through. Swirl in the remaining 1 tablespoon butter. Pour the sauce over the chicken, and serve.

—from the kitchen of Betty Tillman, adapted for crockery-style cooking by Wendy Louise

A Tip from the Kitchen...

If you find your sauces or gravies are coming out too thin, uncover the slow cooker and cook for 15 minutes on high to reduce the liquid and finish the sauce. Color not right? Add some color and flavor enhancers, such as a browning and seasoning sauce or paprika. Enrich your sauce by swirling in one tablespoon of butter at the very end—it's a French twist.

Two Perfect Pork Roasts

#1 The Bachelor's Perfect Pork Roast

Makes 6 to 8 servings

- 1 (3- to 4-pound) pork roast
- 1 medium-sized onion, sliced
- 2 (16-ounce) cans whole berry cranberry sauce

Put the roast in the slow cooker. Surround the roast with the onion. Break up the cranberry sauce and pour it over and around the roast. Cover with the lid and cook on low for 8 to 10 hours, until the roast is very tender. (Or cook on high for about 4 to 6 hours.) Serve the roast smothered in its pot juices with mashed potatoes on the side, or shred and serve the meat as succulent hot pork sandwiches on buns.

#2 Pork Roast Perfection

Makes 6 to 8 servings

- 1 (3- to 4-pound) pork roast
- 2 or 3 garlic cloves, sliced into slivers
- 1 (16-ounce) can whole berry cranberry sauce
- 1 (16-ounce) bottle Catalina-style French salad dressing

Cut pockets in the roast, and insert slivers of garlic. Place the roast in the slow cooker. Pour both the cranberry sauce and the salad dressing over the roast. Cover with the lid and cook on low for 8 to 10 hours, until very tender. Serve with mashed potatoes or buttered flat noodles, or shred the meat for hot meat sandwiches.

A Tip from the Kitchen...

For a Venison Variation—the next time your hunter in the family brings home a venison roast, try this recipe! Omit the garlic-clove slivers and place the venison roast, trimmed of any fat, in the slow cooker. Proceed with the recipe as above. Serve the roast with mashed potatoes and your favorite sides.

Beef in Wine Sauce

Makes 4 to 6 servings

Serve over a rice pilaf or buttered noodles along with crusty French bread and a glass of wine.

- 2 pounds stew meat, cut into 1-inch cubes
- 1 (1.3-ounce) envelope onion soup mix
- 1 (10.5-ounce) can cream of mushroom soup
- 1 (4-ounce) can whole button mushrooms, undrained
- ½ cup dry red wine, port, or sherry

Combine all the ingredients in the slow cooker, mixing together well. Cover with the lid and cook on low for 8 to 10 hours.

—from the kitchen of Lucile Feiereisen, adapted for crockery-style cooking by Wendy Louise

Brook's Beef Burgundy

Makes 6 servings

- 2 slices bacon, chopped
- 1½ pounds beef sirloin tip or round steak, cut into 1-inch cubes
- ½ cup flour for dredging meat
- 1 teaspoon salt
- 1 teaspoon all-purpose seasoned salt
- 1 teaspoon marjoram
- 1 teaspoon thyme
- 1 teaspoon freshly ground black pepper
- 1 clove garlic, minced
- 1 beef bouillon cube, crushed
- 1 cup Burgundy wine
- 1 pound fresh mushrooms, sliced
- 2 tablespoon cornstarch
- Cooked rice, mashed potatoes, or hot buttered noodles for serving

In skillet, cook bacon several minutes until brown. Remove with slotted spoon and set aside. Reserve the drippings.

Meanwhile, dredge the beef with the flour and brown on all sides in drippings. Combine the steak, drippings, bacon, seasonings, bouillon cube, and Burgundy in the slow cooker. Cover with the lid and cook on low for 6 to 8 hours.

Increase the heat to high. Add the mushrooms and cook for 15 minutes. To thicken the sauce, dissolve cornstarch in 2 tablespoons cold water and add to the pot. Stir to blend and continue to cook on high, uncovered, until thickened. Serve with rice, mashed potatoes, or buttered noodles.

A Tip from the Kitchen...

When using lighted candles at the dinner table, choose unscented ones. You don't want the scent of the candle to overpower or conflict with the taste and aroma of your dinner.

Dorothea's French-Style Meat Loaf

Makes 6 to 8 servings

Serve with parsley-buttered new potatoes and a nice vegetable.

- 1½ pounds ground beef
- 1 pound ground cooked or cured ham
- 1 large onion, finely chopped
- ½ cup raisins, soaked, plumped, and drained
- 1 cup dry breadcrumbs
- 2 tablespoons cognac or brandy
- 2 eggs, separated
- ½ teaspoon freshly grated nutmeg
- Salt and freshly ground black pepper, to taste
- 2 tablespoons butter

Gently mix the first 6 ingredients thoroughly. Then add the egg yolks and seasonings, mixing again. Beat the egg whites until stiff and fold into the meat mixture. Form into a loaf and place in a slow cooker sprayed with nonstick vegetable spray. Dot the top of the loaf with the butter. Cover with the lid and cook on low for 8 to 10 hours, or on high for 4 to 5 hours.

—original recipe from the kitchen of Dorothea Loescher, adapted for crockery-style cooking by Wendy Louise

A Tip from the Kitchen...

Separating the eggs and beating the whites stiff before folding into the meat loaf gives a lighter, more delicate loaf.

Rouladen (German Beef Rolls)

Makes 8 servings

This dish requires a bit of prep work, but is well worth it. You can assemble your beef rolls the night before and store them, covered, in the refrigerator. The next day, just take them out, pop them into the slow cooker, and proceed with the recipe. Ask the butcher to slice the meat for you. Or you can buy a flank steak and slice it yourself—total meat weight is approximately 1½ to 2 pounds. Serve with mashed potatoes on the side.

- 8 thin slices of beef round steak, about 4 x 6-inches and ⅛- to ¼-inch thick
- Garlic salt and freshly ground black pepper, to taste
- 1 tablespoon Dijon-style mustard
- 4 slices bacon, sliced in half to make eight 4-inch strips (optional)
- 4 dill pickle spears, cut lengthwise into 8 spears
- 1 small onion, halved and thinly sliced
- 2 tablespoons vegetable oil
- 1 (10.5-ounce) can beef broth
- 1½ teaspoons browning and seasoning sauce
- ¼ cup red wine (optional)
- 1 bay leaf
- 1 tablespoon cornstarch

Lay out each beef slice and lightly season with garlic salt and pepper. Spread lightly with mustard. Lay a bacon slice in center of each steak, if using. Place a pickle spear on top of the bacon. Top with a few thin slices of onion. Roll up each steak around its filling and secure with toothpicks or kitchen string.

Heat the oil in a skillet over medium heat and brown the beef rolls on all sides. Arrange the rolls in the slow cooker. Add the beef broth, browning sauce, and red wine, if using. Add the bay leaf. Cover with the lid and cook on low for 6 to 8 hours, until very tender. Remove the beef rolls to a warm serving platter and cover with foil, leaving the juices in the slow cooker. Remove and discard the bay leaf.

Meanwhile, increase the heat to high. In a small jar, combine the cornstarch with ¼ cup water; cover and shake to

Continued…

soften. Pour mixture into the cooking juices to thicken, stirring to blend. Adjust the seasonings, if needed. Serve the beef rolls drizzled with gravy.

Cook's Note: If you prefer, after putting the beef rolls on the serving platter, you can transfer the cooking juices to a saucepan and make your gravy on the stovetop.

—from the kitchen of Mike Gulan

4-Way Rock Cornish Game Hens

Makes 4 servings

- 4 Rock Cornish game hens, thawed, rinsed, and patted dry
- ¼ stick butter, melted
- 1 (1.3-ounce) envelope onion soup mix
- 1 (12-ounce) jar currant jelly, apricot preserves, orange marmalade, or plum jam (pick one)

Place the game hens in the slow cooker and drizzle the butter over top. Sprinkle the birds evenly with the onion soup mix. Cover with the lid and cook on high for 1 hour. Spoon the jelly over the hens. Cover with the lid, reduce the heat to low, and cook for 6 to 7 hours more, until the hens are falling-off-the-bone tender. Halfway through cooking, lift off the lid and quickly baste the birds again with the jam mixture in the pot; replace the lid and continue cooking.

A Tip from the Kitchen...

Make any day a holiday—think of those Cornish game hens as mini turkeys. Family too small to cook a large turkey? Serve each person their own mini turkey with all the fixings. Alone for the holiday? Cook one up for yourself, or invite a neighbor over and make two. Bake two sweet potatoes in the microwave, open a can of cranberry sauce, add a spiced peach half, and voila, you never even touched your oven!

Game Hens Mexicana

Makes 4 servings

Pass a fruit chutney or refreshing fruit salsa (see following recipe) to garnish the meal.

- 4 Rock Cornish game hens, thawed, rinsed, and patted dry
- ¼ stick butter, melted
- 1 (1.2-ounce) envelope taco seasoning mix
- ½ teaspoon red pepper flakes
- ½ cup canned chicken broth
- Cooked rice, for serving

Place the game hens in the slow cooker and drizzle melted butter over top. Sprinkle the birds evenly with the taco seasoning and red pepper flakes. Gently pour the chicken broth around the hens. Cover with the lid and cook on high for 1 hour; reduce the heat to low and cook for an additional 6 to 7 hours, until the hens are falling-off-the-bone tender. Serve with fluffy cooked rice and Change of Pace Salsa.

A Tip from the Kitchen...

Depending on the size of your slow cooker, you might have trouble squeezing your game hens into the pot. If so, stand them up vertically—shoulders down and legs up in the air!

Change of Pace Salsa

Makes 2-plus cups

- 1 cup finely chopped fresh peaches or nectarines
- 1 cup chopped, seeded cucumber
- 2 green onions, including tops, chopped
- 2 tablespoons snipped parsley
- 1 tablespoon sugar
- 1 tablespoon salad oil
- 1 tablespoon vinegar
- 1 teaspoon grated fresh ginger

Mix all, and chill until serving time. Serve with Game Hens Mexicana.

—from the kitchen of Wendy Louise

Venison Braised with Root Vegetables and Wine

Makes 6 to 8 servings

Here's a recipe for those who have a hunter in the family. The use of onion and the sweetness of the carrots, parsnips, and wine or cola mellow the gaminess of the venison.

- 2 to 3 pounds boneless venison, trimmed of any fat and sliced into 6 to 8 serving-size pieces
- 2 onions, sliced into rings
- 2 to 3 carrots, scrubbed and sliced into strips
- 2 medium parsnips, peeled and sliced into strips
- 1 (1.3-ounce) envelope French onion soup mix
- 1 teaspoon thyme
- 2 cups Marsala wine or 2 cups brown cola soft drink

Place a layer of one-third of the onions in the bottom of the slow cooker; top with half the carrots and half the parsnips. Arrange half the venison slices on top of the vegetables. Sprinkle the meat with half the onion soup mix and ½ teaspoon thyme. Repeat the layering, ending with a top layer of the remaining one-third of the onions. Pour 2 cups Marsala wine around and over all. Cover with the lid and cook on low for 6 to 8 hours, until the venison and root vegetables are tender.

A Tip from the Kitchen...

When cutting the vegetables and meats for slow cooking, cut them to uniform size to ensure even cooking. If cutting beforehand and storing in the refrigerator, always store raw meats separately from vegetables until ready to use. If marinating the meat, use a glass or other nonreactive dish or a plastic bag to avoid acidic interactions between the marinade and the container.

Easy Venison Roast

Makes 8 servings

The slow cooker is a great way to cook wild game to braised tenderness.

- 1 (3-pound) boneless venison roast, trimmed of any fat
- Salt and freshly ground black pepper, to taste
- 1 onion, sliced into rings
- 3 or 4 slices thick-cut smoked bacon, uncooked
- 1 cup apple cider
- 1 (14-ounce) jar brown gravy
- 1 bay leaf

Season the roast liberally with the salt and pepper. Place the onion rings in the bottom of the slow cooker. Lay the roast on the onions. Drape the bacon over the roast. Pour on the cider and gravy. Add the bay leaf. Cover with the lid and cook on low for 8 hours, or until roast is extremely tender. Remove and discard the bay leaf before serving.

Poached Wild Salmon

Makes 4 servings

- 1 small to medium-sized onion, sliced into rings
- 2 stalks celery with leaves, cut into chunks
- 1 lemon, sliced into rounds
- 2 or 3 sprigs fresh parsley, roughly chopped
- 1 bay leaf
- 6 peppercorns
- 4 wild salmon steaks or fillets, about 6 ounces each and cut ¾- to 1-inch thick
- 2 cups lightly salted boiling water
- ½ cup white wine
- Lemon or lime wedges, to pass
- Sea salt, to pass
- Freshly ground black pepper, to pass

Place onion, celery, lemon, and parsley in bottom of slow cooker. Add the bay leaf and peppercorns. Arrange the salmon steaks on top of the bed of vegetables. Pour boiling salted water over and around. Pour in ½ cup white wine. Cover with the lid and cook on low for 2½ to 3 hours, until fish is cooked through, is opaque, and flakes easily, but still holds its shape. Remove salmon from pot to serving plates. (Discard the vegetables and cooking juices.) Pass fresh lemon or lime wedges, coarse sea salt, and freshly cracked black pepper.

Cook's Note: "Fancy up" those salmon servings with one of the following simple toppings:

Easy Hollandaise Sauce

Make according to the directions on a 0.6-ounce Hollandaise sauce seasoning packet and serve warm, drizzled over the fish.

Dill Sauce

- ½ cup mayonnaise
- 1 to 2 tablespoons sour cream
- 2 tablespoons snipped fresh dill or 2 teaspoons dill weed
- 1 tablespoon tarragon vinegar or fresh lemon juice
- Dash salt
- Dash white pepper

Mix in small bowl and pass at serving time to dollop on fish.

Dill-Chive Butter

- ½ stick butter, softened
- 1 teaspoon dried dill
- 1 teaspoon dried parsley
- 2 teaspoons freshly minced chives
- 1 tablespoon fresh lemon juice
- Dash white pepper

Mix together with a fork to blend. Serve over hot fish, to melt and glaze.

Dad's Pheasant or Partridge Dinner

Makes 4 to 6 servings

If you are lucky enough to have somebody who hunts pheasant or partridge in your family, give this Stroganoff-style recipe a try. Mashed potatoes and/or wild rice make nice accompaniments.

- 1 large or 2 smaller pheasants, dressed and quartered, or 2 to 3 partridges, dressed and cut into halves
- Salt and freshly ground black pepper to taste
- Paprika to taste
- 2 tablespoons vegetable oil, or more as needed
- 2 tablespoons butter, or more as needed
- 3 beef bouillon cubes
- 3 cups hot water
- 1 teaspoon Worcestershire sauce
- 1 (8-ounce) box sliced mushrooms, sautéed in butter
- 1 cup sour cream

Season meat with salt, pepper, and paprika. Heat the oil and butter in a large skillet over medium heat, and sauté the pheasant or partridge until browned. (If you have to do it in batches, add more butter and oil between batches.) Remove the meat to the slow cooker. Discard pan drippings from the browning process. Dissolve the bouillon cubes in the hot water. and pour into the slow cooker over and around the birds. Add the Worcestershire sauce. Cover with the lid and cook on low for 5 to 6 hours, or until the meat is falling-off-the-bone tender.

To serve, turn the heat to high, and remove the lid. Remove the meat from the slow cooker, and put into a deep warm serving platter. Tent the meat with foil to keep warm. Fold the mushrooms and their drippings and the sour cream into the sauce in the slow cooker, and stir to blend. Adjust the seasonings , if needed. Continue to heat the sauce, uncovered, for 15 minutes. Pour the sauce over the birds and serve.

—from the kitchen of Paul Tillman

CHAPTER 5

Putting on the Ritz: Parties, Holidays, and Festive Foods

Elaborate entertaining doesn't have to be intimidating when you have your instant butler, your slow cooker, at hand. This makes advanced preparation and stressful timing a cinch, and you will have plenty of time to relax and enjoy your party without being a slave to the kitchen. Slow cookers hold food nicely on the buffet table and make wonderful assistants, maximizing your cooking ability when your oven is filled to capacity—a nice quality during holiday seasons, when you need extra room for that special side dish or second-turkey stuffing that Grandma used to make.

Recipes

- Crab Fondue Appetizer
- The Rush Hour Cook's Easy Chili-Cheese Dip
- Carla's Beef and Refried Bean Dip
- Spunky Salsa
- Captain Jack's Peel 'Em and Eat 'Em Shrimp
- Donna's Slow-Cooker Shrimp Boil
  - Homemade Cocktail Sauce
- Your-Choice Jambalaya
- Paella-Style Shrimp, Chicken, and Sausage Dish
- Trudy's Scalloped Oyster Pudding
- Classic Swiss Fondue
- Brie Cheese Appetizer with Festive Cranberry Chutney
- Everyone's Favorite Party Meatballs
- Cat's Slow-Simmered Meatballs
- Cranberry-'Kraut Meatballs
- Judy B's Seasoned and Simmered Beef for a Crowd

- Slow-Cooked Beef Roast for French Dip Sandwiches
- "Christmas in July"…the Ultimate Turkey Dinner
- Lucile's Crockery Stuffing
- Scalloped Potatoes with Diced Ham for a Crowd
- Vicki's Portable Macaroni and Cheese
- Cheddar Cheese Strata
- Holiday Brisket of Beef with Cranberry-Horseradish Sauce
  - Cranberry-Horseradish Sauce
- Pulled Pork for Sandwiches
  - Lucile's Quick and Easy Coleslaw
- Slow-Cooked Pork Roast 'n Fruit
- Cola-Glazed Ham
- Cheesy Scalloped Potatoes
- Christmas Eve Chili

Crab Fondue Appetizer

Makes 8 to 10 servings

- 1 stick butter, melted
- 1 (16-ounce) package processed cheese, cubed
- 1 cup shredded Cheddar cheese
- 1 (6-ounce) can crabmeat, drained
- Dash sherry, to taste
- Crackers, for dipping

Combine all the ingredients in slow cooker. Cover with the lid and melt into a smooth fondue-style sauce on high. Once blended, reduce the heat to low to keep warm. Serve warm with crackers for dipping.

—from the kitchen of Captain Jack Feiereisen

The Rush Hour Cook's Easy Chili-Cheese Dip

Makes 8 to 10 servings

- 1 (16-ounce) can chili without beans
- 1 (16-ounce) package processed cheese, cubed
- Corn chips or tortilla chips, for dipping
- Red pepper sauce (optional)

Put the chili and cheese in the slow cooker. Cover with the lid and melt on high, stirring occasionally to mix. Reduce the heat to low to keep dip warm while serving. Spice lovers can add red pepper sauce to taste.

—Excerpted from The Rush Hour Cook Presents Effortless Entertaining *by Brook Noel*

Carla's Beef and Refried Bean Dip

Makes 6 cups

I live in "cheese-head" country, and we love to watch the Packer games; we also love our cheese. This is an easy and portable dip that will be a favorite at any football party. Just plug it in and set it on the buffet table for all to enjoy.

- 2 tablespoons vegetable oil
- 1 pound ground beef
- ½ teaspoon salt
- ½ teaspoon garlic powder
- 1 (16-ounce) can refried beans, mashed up with a wooden spoon
- 1 (16-ounce) block packaged processed cheese, diced
- 1 (1.2-ounce) envelope taco seasoning mix
- Multi-colored tortilla chips, for dipping

Heat the oil in a large skillet over medium heat and brown the beef with salt and garlic powder; drain off excess fat. Transfer beef to slow cooker. Add the beans, cheese, and seasoning packet. Cover with the lid and cook on high for 1 hour to melt cheese and heat through; stir to mix. Turn slow cooker to low and continue to heat through serving time. (If mixture is too thick, stir in water, 1 tablespoon at a time, to desired consistency.) Serve warm with tortilla chips for dipping.

—from the kitchen of Carla McGrath

Spunky Salsa

Makes 3 to 4 cups

Not in a slow cooker, but too good to pass up! Serve this no-cook recipe to accent your slow-cooked recipes—great with meats or sandwiches, or just as an appetizer.

- 1 (16-ounce) jar salsa, mild or hot
- 1 (15-ounce) can Mexican corn, drained
- 1 tablespoon sugar
- 1 jalapeño chile, seeded and chopped
- Salt and freshly ground black pepper, to taste

Mix all ingredients together and let sit 30 minutes before serving. Use as an appetizer with tortilla chips or as a contrasting condiment or side garnish to your slow-cooked meats.

—excerpted from The Rush Hour Cook Presents Family Favorites *by Brook Noel*

Captain Jack's Peel 'Em and Eat 'Em Shrimp

Makes 6 to 8 servings

- 3 to 4 pounds fresh shrimp in their shells, #26 to #30 count per pound, or larger
- 1 (12-ounce) bottle beer
- 1 tablespoon salt
- 2 to 3 tablespoons pickling spices or shrimp-boil spices
- Dipping sauces of choice

Rinse the shrimp and put them in the slow cooker. Add the remaining ingredients, mixing well. Cover with the lid and cook on high for 1 to 2 hours, until the shrimp turn pink and are cooked through. Reduce the heat to low and keep shrimp warm during serving. Serve with a favorite condiment, or chill the shrimp and serve cold with cocktail sauce and/or homemade mayonnaise.

—from the kitchen of Captain Jack Feiereisen

A Tip from the Kitchen...

Since we are peeling and eating in rustic fashion, let's get out the finger bowls. Remember those? A nice touch is to serve warmed water with floating lemon slices in little bowls for each of your guests. If you don't want to offer finger bowls, use plenty of good-quality napkins and extra lemon wedges; last but not least, offer moist wipes.

Trudy's Scalloped Oyster Pudding

Makes 6 to 8 servings

Serve as a side dish with your holiday meal or as an elegant first course for a fancy dinner. You may substitute canned oysters for the fresh.

- 1 cup whole milk
- 3 large eggs
- 1 (2 sleeve) box saltine-style crackers, coarsely crumbled (approximately 8 ounces total weight)
- 1 stick butter, melted, plus extra for dotting
- 1½ pints to 1 quart fresh oysters with the liquor

Beat the milk and eggs together in a mixing bowl. Put the crackers into a large bowl and pour the milk mixture over top. Stir in the melted butter. Fold in the oysters and their liquor. Place the mixture in a buttered slow cooker. Dot the top of the pudding with a little butter. Cover with the lid slightly vented and cook the pudding on high for 2 to 4 hours, until set or when a knife inserted in the center comes out clean. Serve warm.

—original recipe by Trudy Pengburn, adapted for crockery-style cooking by Wendy Louise

A Tip from the Kitchen...

If your family has many heirloom recipes, collect them and create several menus as gifts. Add family pictures, journaling, and anecdotes. Print them on attractive paper or take them to a copy store for duplication and binding.

Classic Swiss Fondue

Makes 2 quarts

- 1 clove garlic
- 2 to 3 cups dry Rhine, Chablis, or Riesling wine
- 1 tablespoon lemon juice
- 1 pound Swiss cheese, grated
- ½ pound Cheddar cheese, grated
- 3 tablespoons all-purpose flour
- 3 tablespoons Kirsch
- Freshly ground nutmeg, to taste
- Seasoning salt, to taste
- 1 Italian or French bread loaf, cut into 1-inch cubes

Rub an enameled or stainless steel pan with the garlic. Lightly grease the slow cooker.

In the pan, heat the wine to a simmer and add the lemon juice. Combine cheeses and flour and gradually stir into the wine. Stir constantly until the cheeses have melted. Pour the mixture into the slow cooker. Add the Kirsch and stir well. Sprinkle with nutmeg and seasoning salt. Cover with the lid and cook on high for 30 minutes; reduce the heat to low for 2 to 5 hours. Keep on low while serving. Skewer bite-sized bread cubes onto long forks and dip into warm cheese mixture.

—Recipe contributed by Michael Gulan

Brie Cheese Appetizer with Festive Cranberry Chutney

Makes 8 servings

- 1 round very good Brie cheese
- Festive Cranberry Chutney (see page 219)
- English soda crackers or similar crackers

Variation 1

When serving as a first course, place a wedge of room-temperature Brie on each plate. Serve a very generous portion of Festive Cranberry Chutney (page 219), warm or cold, on the side, along with very good crackers. Let each person assemble to his or her desire.

Variation 2

Place the whole Brie in the oven on a greased oven-proof plate. Bake at 350°F until warmed, softened, and almost on the verge of melting. Top with the chutney and heat 1 to 2 minutes more. Serve warm with good crackers.

—from the kitchen of Wendy Louise

Everyone's Favorite Party Meatballs

Makes 5 dozen

This recipe is best if the meatballs have at least 1 hour to simmer before serving.

- 1 pound ground beef
- ½ cup dry commercial breadcrumbs
- ⅓ cup finely chopped onion
- 1 tablespoon minced parsley
- 1 teaspoon Worcestershire sauce
- 1 teaspoon salt
- ½ teaspoon black pepper
- 1 egg
- 3 tablespoons vegetable oil
- 1 (12-ounce) bottle chili sauce
- 1 (10-ounce) jar grape jelly

Mix the ground beef, breadcrumbs, onion, parsley, seasonings, and egg together. Shape into 1-inch balls.

Heat the oil in a large skillet over medium heat and brown the meatballs for about 10 minutes, turning frequently. Drain off the fat. In the same pan, pour the chili sauce and jelly over the meatballs, stirring until the jelly is melted and the meatballs are coated. Transfer all to a slow cooker. Cover with the lid and cook on low until your guests arrive. Serve warm.

—excerpted from The Rush Hour Cook Presents Effortless Entertaining *by Brook Noel*

Cat's Slow-Simmered Meatballs

Makes 10 to 12 servings

- 3 pounds lean ground beef
- 2 medium-sized eggs
- 1 cup breadcrumbs
- Salt and freshly ground black pepper, to taste
- 3 tablespoons vegetable oil
- 1 (12-ounce) bottle chili sauce
- 1 (16-ounce) can whole berry cranberry sauce
- 1 (12-ounce) can or bottle cranberry juice
- 2 (5.5-ounce) cans spicy Bloody Mary mix

Mix together the beef, eggs, and breadcrumbs. Season with salt and pepper. Form the meat mixture into small meatballs.

Heat the oil in a large skillet over medium heat and brown the meatballs on all sides; drain off excess fat. Transfer the meatballs to the slow cooker. Mix together the chili sauce, cranberry sauce, cranberry juice, and Bloody Mary mix and pour over the meatballs. Cover with the lid and cook on high for about 6 hours.

—*from the kitchen of Cathie Rosemann*

Cranberry-'Kraut Meatballs

Makes about 76 meatballs

- 3 tablespoons vegetable oil
- 1 (38-ounce) bag ready-made frozen meatballs, thawed
- 1 (16-ounce) can whole berry cranberry sauce, broken up
- 1 (16-ounce) can sauerkraut, drained
- 1 (12-ounce) bottle shrimp cocktail sauce
- 2 tablespoons brown sugar

Heat the oil in the skillet over medium heat and brown the meatballs on all sides, if desired. Transfer the meatballs to the slow cooker. Mix together and add the remaining ingredients. Cover with the lid and cook on low for 2 hours, until all the meatballs are heated through and cooked and the flavors have melded.

Cook's Note: Find the meatballs in the frozen food section of your market. They come in 38-ounce bags containing about 76 meatballs per package.

—from the kitchen of June Wallace

"Christmas in July"— The Ultimate Turkey Dinner

Makes 10 to 12 servings

This recipe calls for a turkey slowly cooked and smoked on a covered barbecue grill in the middle of July. The reason we included it was to showcase Lucile's Crockery Stuffing (recipe to follow) and to show the similarities between the slow cooker and the covered-barbecue grill (another slow cooker of sorts). In the stuffing, you might have to substitute canned chestnuts in the summertime or omit them altogether.

- A large turkey, thawed, cleaned, and giblets removed
- Salt and freshly ground black pepper
- A covered, kettle-style barbecue grill
- Hickory bark (chipped and soaked in water)
- 1 recipe Lucile's Crockery Stuffing, page 175

Pat the turkey dry. Season outside and cavity with salt and pepper. Do NOT stuff the turkey when grilling it. Make your stuffing in a slow cooker and serve alongside. Prepare and arrange your coals in a ring around the inside of the barbecue grill. Place a drip pan in the center. Center your turkey over the drip pan to catch all drippings and to keep the fire from flaring up. Sprinkle some of the soaked hickory chips onto the coals. Put the cover on the grill and adjust the cooking vents for a strong, but slow, cooking fire, maintained at about 250 to 275 degrees.

Add more hickory chips periodically and replenish the coals as necessary. Resist opening the cover as much as possible. Cooking time will range from 4 to 6-plus hours, depending on the size of the bird, consistency of fire, and

Continued…

weather variables. Usually, grills come with cooking guidelines and instructions to aid you. Cook until all juices run clear and the meat is literally falling off the bone. A meat thermometer inserted into the thickest part of the bird should read at least 175 degrees (but 180 degrees is considered a safer temperature). The meat should be succulent and very, very tender. Remove the turkey from grill and let set for 30 minutes before carving. Serve with Lucile's Crockery Stuffing (page 175).

Scalloped Potatoes with Diced Ham for a Crowd

Makes 10 to 12 servings

- 2 tablespoons vegetable oil
- 1 pound ham, diced
- 1 large onion, chopped
- 5 pounds potatoes, skins on, washed and sliced
- ½ cup margarine
- ½ cup all-purpose flour
- 4 cups whole milk
- 1 pound yellow cheese, such as Cheddar, grated
- Salt and freshly ground black pepper, to taste

Heat the oil in a large skillet over medium heat and sauté the ham and onion until the onion is transparent. Put them in a large slow cooker. Add the potatoes to the slow cooker and stir to combine.

Heat the margarine in the skillet, and when it is melted and bubbly, whisk in the flour to make a roux. Heat to the boiling point and add the milk, mixing constantly with wire whisk until thickened. Fold in the cheese and stir until smooth. Add the salt and pepper. Pour over the potato-ham mixture and mix well. Cover with the lid, and cook on low for 7 to 8 hours, until bubbly and the potatoes are tender.

—*excerpted and adapted from* Frozen Assets: Cook for a Day and Eat for a Month *with Deborah Taylor-Hough*

Vicki's Portable Macaroni and Cheese

Makes 10 servings

This versatile recipe comes to us courtesy of Vicki in Madison, Wisconsin. Vicki writes, "This recipe has long been a favorite of my co-workers for our monthly potluck lunches. The short assembly time means I can prepare it at home, plug it in when I arrive at work, and 4 hours later, it is ready to join the huge spread of other foods. To make it heartier, I have added diced celery, onions, and ham upon occasion."

- 1 (16-ounce) package elbow macaroni, cooked and drained
- ½ cup butter or margarine
- ½ cup all-purpose flour
- 2 teaspoons salt
- 4 cups whole milk
- 1 (16-ounce) block processed cheese, cubed
- Paprika, to taste

Melt the butter in a saucepan. Stir in the flour. Gradually stir in the milk; continue stirring until thickened. Add the cheese, a few pieces at a time, and stir until completely melted. Combine the macaroni and the cheese sauce in a large slow cooker. Sprinkle with paprika. Cover with the lid and cook on low for 4 hours.

—from the kitchen of Vicki Lanzendorf

A Tip from the Kitchen...

Wouldn't Vicki's macaroni be a great dish to take to any holiday pot-luck party—especially if kids are involved! It always seems like there is never anything good for kids to eat, amongst all the fancy holiday fare gracing the table—and it never fails, your picky eaters will go home hungry. Serve this for the kids, and you'll be the hit of the party!

Cheddar Cheese Strata

Makes 8 to 10 servings

Serve as a light dinner with a side salad or serve as a hearty side dish.

- 12 slices white bread
- Very soft butter, for spreading (about 4 tablespoons)
- 3 cups shredded Cheddar cheese
- 5 large eggs
- 3 cups heated whole milk
- 2 tablespoons Worcestershire sauce
- 1 teaspoon dry mustard
- ½ teaspoon salt
- ¼ to ½ teaspoon cayenne, or 2 to 3 dashes hot sauce

Lightly butter the bread slices, and cube them. Spray the slow cooker with nonstick cooking spray. Place half the bread cubes in the slow cooker. Top with half the cheese. Repeat the layers with the remaining bread and cheese.

Combine the eggs, milk, and seasoning in a bowl and beat with a fork until well blended. Pour over the layers in the slow cooker. Gently press down the layers to absorb the milk mixture. Cover with the lid and cook on high for 1 hour; reduce the heat to low and cook for 3 to 4 more hours, until the pudding has set.

When the strata is cooked, turn off the heat, remove the lid, and let the strata sit for 10 minutes before serving.

—from the kitchen of Captain Jack

Holiday Brisket of Beef with Cranberry-Horseradish Sauce

Makes 8 to 10 servings

Serve hot and thinly sliced, accompanied by parsleyed and buttered new potatoes and Cranberry-Horseradish Sauce.

- 1 (3- to 4-pound) center-cut beef brisket, trimmed of excess fat
- Bottled smoke, to taste
- Onion salt, to taste
- Garlic salt, to taste
- Celery salt, to taste
- 4 to 6 black peppercorns
- 1½ cups barbecue sauce
- Cranberry-Horseradish Sauce (recipe follows)

Add liberal amounts of smoke and salts to both sides of the brisket, rubbing in well. Put the brisket in the slow cooker. Add about ½ cup water and the peppercorns. Cover with the lid and cook on low for 8 to 10 hours, until the beef is fork tender. During the last hour of cooking, add the barbecue sauce. Serve with Cranberry-Horseradish Sauce.

—from the kitchen of Auntie Joan

Cranberry-Horseradish Sauce

Makes 6 servings

- 1 (16-ounce) can whole berry cranberry sauce
- 2 tablespoons butter
- 2 tablespoons brown sugar
- 2 tablespoons horseradish
- 1 teaspoon Dijon-style mustard

Heat all the ingredients together in a large saucepan until the butter and brown sugar are melted and all the ingredients are incorporated. Serve warm or cold as an accompaniment to meats; especially good with turkey, pork, or beef brisket.

—from the kitchen of Auntie Joan

A Tip from the Kitchen...

Turn your slow cooker into a simmering potpourri pot. Stud some oranges with whole cloves, add a couple of cinnamon sticks, some star anise, and some water, and simmer away. Let the scents of the season fill your house with aromatic comfort. Just be careful not to scorch the pot, since you are doing this with the cover off.

Pulled Pork for Sandwiches

Makes 8 to 10 servings

- 1 (3- to 4-pound) pork roast
- 1 (10.5-ounce) can chicken broth or 1 (12-ounce) bottle beer
- 3 or 4 garlic cloves, left whole
- 1 (16-ounce) bottle favorite barbecue sauce
- Salt and freshly ground black pepper, to taste
- Toasted buns, for serving
- Coleslaw, for serving

Place the pork roast in the slow cooker. Add broth and the garlic cloves. Cover with the lid and cook for 8 to 10 hours, until the roast can be shredded with a fork. Remove the roast, juices, and garlic from the slow cooker. Shred, or pull, the meat and return it to the slow cooker. Mix with the barbecue sauce and season with salt and pepper. Return some cooking juices if the meat mixture seems too thick. Continue to cook until all is heated through. Serve piled on toasted buns and topped with crispy coleslaw (recipe follows).

—from the kitchen of Captain Jack

Lucile's Quick and Easy Coleslaw

Serving sizes variable

I call this "magic" coleslaw because it comes together so quickly, and amounts used are totally up to your taste.

- Shredded cabbage
- Shredded carrots
- Cream or half-and-half (½ to ¾ cup)
- Cider vinegar (1 to 2 tablespoons)
- Pinch sugar
- Salt and freshly ground black pepper, to taste
- Dusting paprika, for color

Place shredded cabbage and carrots in a serving bowl. In a second bowl, stir together the cream and vinegar until thickened. Add the sugar, salt, and pepper. Pour, as desired, over the shredded vegetables and toss to coat. Dust the finished slaw with paprika and refrigerate until serving time. Serve as a side dish or as a topping on Pulled Pork Sandwiches.

—from the kitchen of my mother-in-law

Slow-Cooked Pork Roast 'n Fruit

Makes 8 to 10 servings

- 1 (3- to 4-pound) pork roast
- 1 tablespoon vegetable oil
- Salt and freshly ground black pepper, to taste
- 8 ounces mixed dried fruit
- 1 onion, cut into wedges
- 8 ounces apple juice or water
- ½ teaspoon allspice

Rub the meat all over with cooking oil and season with salt and pepper. Heat a large skillet over medium heat and brown the roast on all sides. Transfer the roast to the slow cooker. In the same skillet, sauté the dried fruit, onion, apple juice, and allspice for 1 or 2 minutes. Pour the mixture over the roast. Cover with the lid and cook on low for 8 to 10 hours or until very tender.

CHAPTER 6

Side Dishes to Round Out Your Meal

Thirty reasons not to overlook our fruits and vegetables.

Recipes

- A Really Good Ratatouille
- Olives Steeped in Wine
- Roasted Root Vegetable Side Dish
- Braised Onions
- Corn on the Cob
- Beans, Beans, Beans
- Auntie Mae's "Baked" Acorn or Butternut Squash
- Green Bean Side Dish
- The Rush Hour Cook's Ravishing Vegetable Medley
- MaryAnn's "Baked" Vegetable Dish
- Tammy's Hot Vegetable Casserole
- Old-Fashioned Stewed Tomatoes with Zucchini
- Slow-Cooker Risotto
- "Baked" Potatoes

- Baby Reds
- Aunt Sally's Potatoes
- Easy Ranch Potato Side Dish
- Parsleyed Boiled New Potatoes
- The Rush Hour Cook's Dijon Potatoes
- Bonnie's Hot German Potato Salad
- A Sweet Potato Casserole
- Samantha's Favorite Cornbread Pudding
- Fancy Wild Rice
- Fancy Pickled Button Mushrooms
- Hot Fruit Compote
- Lucile's Homemade Applesauce
- Cola-Spiced Apple Rings
- Festive Cranberry Chutney
- Cranberry-Pear Relish
- Alsace–Lorraine Apple Butter

A Really Good Ratatouille

Makes 6 to 8 servings

This is an excellent side dish served warm with lamb or grilled meats, or served cold as a salad or first course. This keeps up to one week in the refrigerator.

- ¼ to ⅓ cup olive oil
- 1 large onion, diced
- 1 green pepper, cut into bite-sized pieces
- 3 cloves garlic, minced
- 1 large eggplant, peeled and cut into bite-sized pieces
- 1 large zucchini, unpeeled and sliced into medallions
- 4 to 6 tomatoes, peeled and chopped, or 2 (14.5-ounce) cans peeled whole tomatoes, broken up
- 12 large black olives, pitted and halved
- 1 bay leaf
- Thyme, to taste
- Salt and freshly ground black pepper, to taste

Heat the oil in a large nonstick skillet over medium heat and sauté the onion until golden. Add the green pepper and garlic, and stir. Add the eggplant and zucchini, mixing well. Continue to cook for 5 minutes. Transfer the vegetables to the slow cooker and add the tomatoes, black olives, and seasonings. Gently toss to mix well. Cover with the lid and cook on high for 2 to 3 hours, until the vegetables are tender but still hold their shape.

—from the kitchen of Auntie Joan

Olives Steeped in Wine

Makes 3 cups

In my travels through Europe, almost every meal (except breakfast) without fail was accompanied by a little bowl of mixed cured olives. When we'd get home, I'd tease my sister that I was going through olive-withdrawal. Here is an exotic little recipe to serve as an appetizer or side condiment with almost any meal.

- 1 cup brine-cured black olives with pits, drained and juice reserved
- 2 cups brine-cured Mediterranean-mixed olives with pits, drained and juice reserved
- ¾ cup dry red wine
- 1 tablespoon extra virgin olive oil
- 1 tablespoon reserved olive juice
- ¼ teaspoon fennel seeds, crushed
- 2 to 4 garlic cloves, crushed but left whole
- 1 or 2 sprigs of fresh rosemary

Mix the olives, wine, olive oil, olive juice, and fennel seeds and put in the slow cooker. Tuck in the garlic and rosemary. Cover with the lid and cook on low for 1½ to 2½ hours, until the olives are plumped and the flavors have blended. Cool slightly and serve warm, or store in sterilized jar in the refrigerator. If chilled, serve the olives at room temperature.

—from the kitchen of Wendy Louise

Roasted Root Vegetable Side Dish

Makes 8 to 10 side servings

- 3 cups peeled and cubed turnips (about 2 turnips)
- 3 cups peeled and cubed sweet potato (about 1 large sweet potato)
- 2½ cups peeled and cubed Granny Smith apples
- 1 cup peeled and cubed parsnip (about 1 medium-sized parsnip)
- 1 cup dried cranberries
- ½ cup dark brown sugar
- 1 tablespoon lemon juice
- 2 tablespoons butter, melted
- Juice from 1 orange

Spray the slow cooker with nonstick cooking spray. Put all the ingredients, except the orange juice, in the slow cooker and stir to mix. Cover with the lid and cook on low for 5 to 6 hours, or on high for 3 hours, until the vegetables are fork tender but still hold their shape. Just before serving, stir in the orange juice. Serve hot.

—from the kitchen of June Wallace

Braised Onions

Makes 6 to 8 servings

Serve as a side dish with roasted or grilled meats.

- 2 tablespoons butter
- 6 to 8 medium to large sweet onions, peeled and both ends trimmed
- 1 cup vegetable broth, chicken broth, or white or red wine mixed with a little water
- Salt and freshly ground black pepper, to taste

Heat the butter in a skillet over medium heat and sauté the whole onions until well glazed and golden. Spray the slow cooker with nonstick cooking spray. Place the onions side by side in the slow cooker. Pour on the broth or wine with water. Cover with the lid and cook on low for 10 hours. If necessary, remove the lid toward the end of cooking time to reduce the liquid and to caramelize the sauce.

—from the kitchen of Great-Aunt Louise

A Tip from the Kitchen...

Quick garnishes on a plate or platter make a colorful statement— and another course! Choose spiced peaches, ruby-red crabapples, sliced fresh pineapple, gingered pears, sliced kiwi, clusters of mini purple grapes, pickled mushrooms, a dollop of coarsely cut salsa cruda relish, chutney, pickled kumquats, a sliced tomato from your garden, or even nasturtium blossoms—the list is endless. Browse the fancy-food section of your market and get creative, or take a stroll through your garden to pick something sun-ripened and homegrown.

Corn on the Cob

Serve with Caleb's Brats 'N Beer (page 104)

Select freshly picked ears of corn. Pull back
the husks and remove the silk. Replace
husks back around the corn kernels. Trim
off excess stalks to make level bottoms.
Stand the ears upright in the slow cooker.
Pour in ½ to 1 cup water. Cover with the
lid and steam on low for 2 to 3 hours.
Pull back the husks, slather with butter,
and sprinkle with salt and pepper. Eat
immediately!

—from the kitchen of Caleb Feiereisen

Beans, Beans, Beans

Makes 12 servings

- 4 strips thick bacon, uncooked
- 1 (31-ounce) can baked beans
- 1 (16-ounce) can kidney beans
- 1 (16-ounce) can black beans
- 1 (16-ounce) can butter beans
- 1 (16-ounce) can lima beans
- 1 (16-ounce) can navy beans
- 1 onion, finely chopped
- 2 to 3 tablespoons brown sugar
- ½ cup catsup
- ½ tablespoon minced garlic or garlic powder
- 1 teaspoon black pepper

Lay bacon strips on bottom of slow cooker. Mix the remaining ingredients together in a mixing bowl and add to the slow cooker. Cover with the lid and cook on low for 6 to 8 hours. Serve hot.

—from the kitchen of "Miz Malibu"

Auntie Mae's "Baked" Acorn or Butternut Squash

Makes 4 servings

- 1 acorn or butternut squash, quartered
- 4 tablespoons butter
- 4 tablespoons brown sugar
- ¼ teaspoon ground nutmeg
- Salt and freshly ground black pepper, to taste

Cut the squash into uniform serving-sized pieces, and remove the seeds. Do not peel. Dab each piece with butter and brown sugar and sprinkle with a dusting of nutmeg. Wrap individually in foil and stack in the slow cooker. Do not add any water. Cover with the lid and cook on high for 5 hours, or on low for 6 to 8 hours. Carefully remove them from the slow cooker; carefully remove the foil and season with salt and pepper. Serve warm.

—from the kitchen of Mae Perdue

Green Bean Side Dish

Makes 6 servings

- 1 (16-ounce) bag frozen green beans, thawed
- 1 small onion, finely chopped
- 1 (10.75-ounce) can cream of mushroom soup
- ½ cup milk or white wine
- 2 teaspoons Worcestershire sauce
- 1 (2.8-ounce) can French-fried onions

Spray the slow cooker with nonstick cooking spray. Combine the first 5 ingredients, blending well, and put mixture into the slow cooker. Cover with the lid and cook on low for 4 to 5 hours. Just before serving, sprinkle with the onions. (You can crisp the onions in the oven, if desired, before sprinkling on casserole.)

—*from the kitchen of Wendy Louise*

The Rush Hour Cook's Ravishing Vegetable Medley

Makes 8 servings

- 1 cup cut-up zucchini
- 1 cup cut-up carrots
- 1 cup cut-up broccoli
- 1 cup cut-up cauliflower
- 1 cup cut-up onion
- 1 cup cut-up green pepper
- 1 cup cut-up yellow squash
- ¼ cup olive oil
- 2 tablespoons red wine vinegar (optional)
- 2 tablespoons minced garlic
- 1 tablespoon oregano
- 1 tablespoon pepper
- 1 teaspoon salt

Put the vegetables into the slow cooker. Mix the remaining ingredients together, and toss with the vegetables to coat evenly. Cover with the lid and cook on high for about 2 hours, until the vegetables are fork tender but firm, adding a little water, if necessary. Stir once halfway through cooking. Serve warm.

—excerpted and adapted from The Rush Hour Cook Presents Effortless Entertaining *by Brook Noel*

MaryAnn's "Baked" Vegetable Dish

Makes 6 to 8 servings

- 8 ounces frozen broccoli, thawed
- 8 ounces frozen cauliflower, thawed
- 8 ounces mixed frozen vegetables, thawed
- 1 (6- to 8-ounce) jar processed cheese spread
- 1 (10.75-ounce) can cream of mushroom soup
- 1 (10.75-ounce) can cream of broccoli soup
- 1 (6-ounce) can onion rings

Put all the vegetables except onion rings in slow cooker. Mix the cheese spread with the soups and pour over vegetables. Cover with the lid and cook on high for 3 hours. Top with the onion rings; cover with the lid and cook on high for 1 more hour.

—from the kitchen of MaryAnn Koopmann

Tammy's Hot Vegetable Casserole

Makes 6 to 8 servings

- 1 (16-ounce) package frozen broccoli, thawed
- 1 (10.75-ounce) can cream of mushroom soup
- ¼ cup chopped onion
- 1 ⅓ cups uncooked minute-style rice
- 1 (8-ounce) jar processed cheese spread
- 1 (8-ounce) can sliced water chestnuts, drained

Spray the slow cooker with nonstick cooking spray. Mix the first 5 ingredients together in the slow cooker. Cover with the lid and cook on high for 3 hours. Add the water chestnuts for last 45 minutes of cooking, so they will be crisp yet tender.

—from the kitchen of MaryAnn Koopmann

A Tip from the Kitchen...

Making a side dish or vegetable casserole? Don't have room in the oven? Make it in your slow cooker instead and keep it warm while you are cooking everything else. The General Rule of Thumb for Conversion: slow cooking equals 1 hour of conventional cooking multiplied by 2 for high setting or multiplied by 4 for low setting.

Old-Fashioned Stewed Tomatoes with Zucchini

Makes 8 to 10 servings

Serve the stewed vegetables warm, as a side dish in little bowls. Let each person salt and pepper his or her portion to their taste.

- 2 medium-sized zucchini, cleaned, unpeeled, and sliced into discs
- 1 small onion, chopped
- 2 (14.5-ounce) cans stewed whole tomatoes with juice
- 1 teaspoon crushed dried basil

Place all in the slow cooker, cover with the lid, and cook on low or high until the zucchini are tender but still hold their shape. Break up the tomatoes lightly with a fork at the end of cooking.

—from the kitchen of Great-Aunt Louise

Slow-Cooker Risotto

Makes 4 to 6 servings

- 1 tablespoon butter
- 1 tablespoon olive oil
- ¼ cup minced shallots
- 1 cup Arborio rice
- 2 cups chicken broth
- ⅓ cup dry white wine (or use more chicken broth)
- 1 pinch saffron (optional)
- Sea salt
- White pepper
- ½ cup freshly grated Parmigiano-Reggiano cheese

Heat the butter and oil in a large skillet over medium heat. Sauté the shallots for 4 to 5 minutes. Add the rice and stir to coat. Spray the slow cooker with nonstick cooking spray and transfer the mixture to the slow cooker. Add the chicken broth, 1 cup water, wine, and saffron, stirring well. Cover with the lid and cook on high until the rice is tender, all the liquid has been absorbed, and the mixture is creamy, 2 to 3 hours. Before serving, season with salt and white pepper and toss with Parmigiano-Reggiano cheese. Serve hot.

Parsleyed Boiled New Potatoes

Makes 6 to 8 servings

Serve warm as a side dish.

- 1 to 2 pounds medium-sized red potatoes
- Melted butter, to taste
- Fresh parsley, minced
- Salt and freshly ground black pepper, to taste

Pare a strip of peel from around the middle of each potato. Place the potatoes and ¼ to ½ cup water in the slow cooker. Cover with the lid and cook on high for 1½ to 3 hours, until fork tender. Timing will depend on the size of the potatoes. (You can add a little lemon juice to the water to preserve color. Potatoes have a tendency to darken over prolonged cooking or holding time.) At serving time, drain and toss the potatoes with the butter, fresh parsley, salt, and pepper.

—from the kitchen of Hannalorre

The Rush Hour Cook's Dijon Potatoes

Makes 8 servings

- 5 tablespoons butter
- 5 tablespoons all-purpose flour
- 2½ cups whole milk
- ½ to ¾ cup Dijon-style mustard, or to taste
- 8 baking potatoes, peeled and thinly sliced
- 1 cup shredded Swiss cheese
- Salt and white pepper, to taste

Heat the butter in a saucepan over medium heat, and when it is melted and bubbly, whisk in the flour to make a roux. Slowly add the milk, stirring all the while. Cook gently until the sauce thickens. Stir in the mustard. Set aside.

Spray the slow cooker with nonstick cooking spray. Place the sliced potatoes into the slow cooker. Pour the sauce over the potatoes, and stir to mix. Cover with the lid and cook on high for 1 hour; reduce the heat to low and cook for 4 hours more, until potatoes are tender. Sprinkle the Swiss cheese on the top, cover with the lid, and continue to cook until cheese has melted. Adjust seasoning with salt and white pepper if desired.

—excerpted and adapted from the kitchen of Brook Noel

Bonnie's Hot German Potato Salad

Makes 10 servings

- 4 to 6 slices thick-cut bacon, diced
- 1 small to medium red onion, chopped
- 6 long white potatoes (need about 1½ to 2 pounds), sliced just under ¼-inch thick
- 2 stalks celery, sliced
- ½ green bell pepper, diced
- ¼ cup cider vinegar
- 2 tablespoons water
- 2 tablespoons sugar
- 1 teaspoon all-purpose seasoning salt
- ½ teaspoon dry mustard
- ½ teaspoon celery seed
- ¼ cup chopped fresh parsley

Sauté the bacon until browned and crisp. Remove to paper towels to drain and set aside. Reserve 2 tablespoons bacon drippings in skillet. In the drippings, cook the onion 5 minutes. Toss the onion and drippings with the potato slices and put in slow cooker. Combine vinegar, water, sugar, seasoning salt, dry mustard, and celery seed; pour over potatoes and gently stir to mix. Cover with the lid and cook on low for 6 to 8 hours, until the potatoes are fork tender but still hold their shape. Fold in the reserved bacon and the parsley before serving and adjust seasonings, as needed. Serve warm.

—from the kitchen of Mike Gulan

A Sweet Potato Casserole

Makes 6 to 8 servings

- 2 (16-ounce) cans sweet potatoes or yams, drained and mashed
- ½ cup fresh orange juice or apple juice
- 4 tablespoons (½ stick) butter, melted
- 1 teaspoon grated orange peel
- ¼ teaspoon allspice or pumpkin pie spice
- Salt and white pepper, to taste
- 2 large eggs, well beaten

Beat the yams with all the ingredients, except the eggs, until smooth and blended. Fold in the eggs.

Spray the slow cooker with nonstick cooking spray. Transfer potato mixture into the slow cooker. Cover with the lid and cook on high for 1 hour; reduce the heat to low and cook for 3 to 4 hours more. Serve as a side dish for holiday meals.

—from the kitchen of Wendy Louise

Fancy Pickled Button Mushrooms

Makes 8 to 10 servings

- 1 to 2 pounds firm white button mushrooms, stems trimmed flush with caps
- 1 red onion, minced or finely diced
- 1 to 2 cloves garlic, smashed and minced
- ½ cup cider or tarragon vinegar
- ½ cup olive oil
- 1 to 2 cups white wine
- 1 teaspoon mixed pickling spices
- 1 or 2 bay leaves
- Several whole black peppercorns
- ½ teaspoon salt

Put all the ingredients in the slow cooker, and cover with the lid. Cook on high for 1 to 3 hours, until the mushrooms are pickled but tender-firm. Store, refrigerated, in sterilized jars. Serve cold as an appetizer or with cocktails.

—from the kitchen of Wendy Louise

Hot Fruit Compote

Makes 6 to 8 servings

This side dish makes an elegant accompaniment for chicken, turkey, and wild game, and is very easy to make—as there is no critical timing involved. You may also assemble the dish the night before and warm it on the day of serving, a nice feature during the busy holiday season. Save all the fruit juices for use in a gelatin mold or to replace milk in a cake recipe.

- 1 (20-ounce) can pineapple rings
- 1 (15-ounce) can peaches
- 1 (14-ounce) jar apple rings
- 1 (15-ounce) can pears
- 1 (15-ounce) can apricots
- 1 stick butter
- ½ cup firmly packed brown sugar
- 2 tablespoons all-purpose flour
- 1 cup sherry or 1 cup drained juice from the fruits

Drain all the fruits, reserving the juice for another recipe (or use in place of the sherry in this recipe). Arrange the fruits in any order in a buttered slow cooker.

Heat the butter in the top of a double boiler and stir in the sugar and flour, cooking and stirring constantly until blended and smooth. Stir in the sherry, making a smooth sauce. Pour the sauce over the fruits in the slow cooker. Cover with the lid and cook on high for 1 to 3 hours to meld flavors and heat through. Reduce the heat to low to hold for serving. Serve the compote warm and bubbling alongside your favorite entrée.

—from the kitchen of Wendy Louise

Festive Cranberry Chutney

Makes 2 quarts

Serve at room temperature, as a condiment for grilled meats or as an accompaniment for soft cheeses, such as the Brie Cheese Appetizer (page 167).

- 2 pounds fresh whole cranberries
- 10 whole cloves
- 2 (3-inch) cinnamon sticks
- ¼ teaspoon salt
- ¼ cup cider vinegar
- 1½ cups sugar
- ¼ cup water
- 1½ cups dark raisins
- 1 (10-ounce) package chopped dates
- 1 to 2 tablespoons orange-flavored liqueur (optional)

Combine first 7 ingredients in slow cooker. Cover with the lid and cook on low for 4 hours, until the cranberries have popped and the mixture thickens. Remove the lid and stir in the dates and raisins. Turn the heat to high and cook, vented, for 1 hour more. Stir in the orange liqueur, if using. The chutney should be quite thick and the dates chewy. Remove the cinnamon sticks and ladle the mixture into hot, sterilized canning jars. Immediately screw on the lids. Cool on the kitchen counter. Once cooled, store in the refrigerator.

—from the kitchen of Wendy Louise

A Tip from the Kitchen...

Chutneys are great for holiday gift-giving and hostess gifts instead of the usual bottle of wine. Decorate the jar and give the hostess serving suggestions included with the gift.

Cranberry-Pear Relish

Makes 8 servings

- 1 pound fresh cranberries
- 2 cups sugar
- 1 tart apple, peeled and chopped
- 1 pear, chopped
- 1 teaspoon ground cinnamon
- 1 teaspoon ground ginger
- 1 teaspoon grated orange zest
- 1 teaspoon grated lemon zest
- ½ cup chopped walnuts (optional)

Put the cranberries, 1 cup water, and sugar into the slow cooker. Cover with the lid and cook on high until the cranberries are plumped and popped. Add the apple, pear, spices, and zests. Cover with the lid and cook 30 to 45 minutes more to blend flavors. Do not let the apple and pear become too soft—as this is more a relish than a sauce. Fold in the chopped walnuts, if using. Cool or refrigerate for up to 1 week. Serve as a cold relish, or with the Brie Cheese Appetizer, page 167.

—from the kitchen of Auntie Joan

A Tip from the Kitchen...

You may store any of these chutneys, relishes, and compotes in sterilized jars in your pantry or refrigerator—and these are great for gift-giving. Immediately ladle your recipe while piping hot into sterilized jars and promptly screw on self-sealing caps. As the jars cool, the caps will indent, forming a proper seal. Before filling, your jars may be sterilized in the dishwasher, or the old-fashioned way—placed upside-down in a saucepan filled with about 1 inch of boiling water and sterilized on the stove top for about 10 minutes.

Literally boil and steam the jars—throw the caps in there, too, and your ladle—for about 10 minutes just prior to filling. Using tongs, carefully remove the hot jars from the water bath and invert them on paper towels. The steam and water droplets will automatically evaporate from the jars, leaving clean, dry interiors. Proceed with filling, wiping any drips and spills from the rims, so you have a clean seal. Immediately screw tops on jars. Let the filled jars cool undisturbed on the kitchen counter. I know this sounds like quite the process, but it's really fun—and once you've done it, you'll be a pro. Add decorations and serving suggestions on little tags with your gifts.

Alsace-Lorraine Apple Butter

Makes 6 to 10 pints

- 4 quarts finely chopped tart cooking apples
- 2 cups apple cider
- 3 cups sugar
- 3 teaspoons ground cinnamon
- ½ teaspoon ground cloves (optional)
- Pinch of salt

Put the ingredients in slow cooker in the order listed. Stir to blend. Cover with the lid and cook on high for 3 hours, stirring occasionally. Reduce the heat to low and continue to cook, covered but vented with a toothpick, for 10 to 12 hours more, stirring occasionally. The butter is done when it reduces to a thickened jam with dark brown color. Pour into hot sterilized jars (see page 221) and seal immediately. Store in a cool, dark place. Serve on crumpets or slather on scones.

—from the kitchen of Great-Aunt Louise

CHAPTER 7

The Finishing Touches:
Desserts and Beverages

Dessert time is the perfect time to receive a standing ovation with a memorable dessert, served warm and bubbling from your slow cooker—a grand finale to your perfectly orchestrated meal!

Recipes

- Cheryl's Sherried Pears with Crème Fraîche
  - Crème Fraîche
- Slow-Cooker "Baked" Apples
- Caramel-Baked Apples
- Mother's Glazed Dessert Peaches
- Baked Cherry-Almond Dessert
- Old-Fashioned Tapioca Pudding
- Cherries Jubilee
- Strawberry Delight
- Bonnie's Stewed Rhubarb Compote
- Mixed Dried-Fruit Dessert Compote
- Mocha Fondue
- The Rush Hour Cook's Fondue for You
- Devilish Chocolate Cake Dessert
  - Butter Pecan Variation

- Lemon Cake with Summer Berries
  - Orange Dream Cake with Strawberries
- Dessert Dipped Strawberries
- Mother's Bread Pudding
- June Wallace's Rice Pudding
- The Story Lady's Sweet Caramel Custard
- Kid's Favorite Hot Chocolate
  - Mocha-Flavored Variation
- Mulled Juice 'n Tea Punch
- Mulled Wine
- Andy's Mulled Cider
- Dipped Jellied Candies

Cheryl's Sherried Pears with Crème Fraîche

Serving suggestion: 1 pear (2 halves) per person

- Winter pears, such as Bosc, peeled, halved, and cored
- Butter
- Strawberry jam
- Brown sugar
- Macaroons, crumbled
- Sherry or water

Grease the inside of the slow cooker. Arrange the halved, peeled, and cored winter pears, cored-side up, in the slow cooker. Dot the center of each layered pear half with butter, a dab of strawberry jam, a pinch of brown sugar, and a dab of crumbled macaroons, if using. Sprinkle with a little sherry. Cover with the lid and cook on low for 1 to 3 hours, until the pears are fork tender but still hold their shape. Add a little more sherry or water only if necessary.

To serve, place 2 pear halves on a dessert plate and garnish with additional crumbled macaroons and any of the remaining cooking juices. Serve warm with a garnish of whipped cream, sour cream, ice cream of your choice, or Crème Fraîche (recipe follows).

—*from the kitchen of Cheryl Adams*

Crème Fraîche (to go with Cheryl's Sherried Pears on previous page)

Not only for desserts, crème fraîche has an additional advantage over sour cream in that it can be boiled, simmered, and reduced with little risk of its curdling in heated sauces.

- 1 cup heavy cream
- 2 tablespoons buttermilk or yogurt

Combine ingredients in a glass container and let sit at room temperature for 5 to 8 hours or overnight to thicken. Use instead of sour cream on desserts or in sauces. Once the crème fraîche has set, you can refrigerate it for up to 1 week in a covered glass container.

Slow-Cooker "Baked" Apples

Makes 4 to 6 servings

- 4 to 6 tart cooking apples
- 2 to 3 tablespoons raisins
- ¼ cup brown sugar
- ½ teaspoon ground cinnamon
- ¼ teaspoon ground nutmeg
- 1 to 2 tablespoons butter, for dotting
- Half-and-half, for serving

Core apples and pare a strip of peel off the top of each apple. Nestle the apples, side by side, in the slow cooker. Mix together the raisins, brown sugar, cinnamon, and nutmeg. Fill the center of each apple. Dot each with butter. Pour ½ cup water around the apples. Cover with the lid and cook on low for 2 to 4 hours, until the apples are tender but still hold their shape. Carefully spoon into dessert bowls and serve warm. Pass the half-and-half to pour over apples.

Cook's Note: Check apples at 3 hours—they might be done. The apples may also be served with vanilla ice cream.

—from the kitchen of Betty Tillman

Cherries Jubilee

Makes 4 to 8 servings

- 1 or 2 (16-ounce) cans pitted dark sweet cherries, drained with juice reserved
- 1 or 2 tablespoons cornstarch
- ¼ cup brandy
- Vanilla ice cream, for serving

Place the drained cherries in the slow cooker. Dissolve the cornstarch in the reserved cherry juice and pour over the cherries. Cover with the lid and cook on low until the sauce is thickened and cherries are heated through. When ready to serve, ignite ¼ cup brandy in a ladle. When the flames die down, pour brandy onto the cherry mixture and gently incorporate. Serve the sauce warm over rich vanilla ice cream in your fanciest dessert bowls or stemmed glasses.

—from the kitchen of Wendy Louise

Strawberry Delight

Makes 6 servings

- 1 (21-ounce) can strawberry pie filling
- ½ teaspoon vanilla extract
- 1 (18.25-ounce) box yellow cake mix
- ½ cup melted butter
- ¼ cup chopped nuts (optional)
- Sweetened heavy whipped cream
- Fresh strawberries, for garnish

Mix the pie filling with the vanilla extract, and pour into the slow cooker. Mix together the cake mix and melted butter and stir until crumbly. Sprinkle over the pie filling. Top with nuts, if using. Cover with the lid and cook on low 3 to 4 hours. Scoop into dessert bowls and serve warm, topped with sweetened whipped cream. Garnish with a fresh strawberry.

Cook's Note: For an extra treat, add 1 cup diced fresh rhubarb and 2 tablespoons brown sugar to the strawberry pie filling before putting it in the slow cooker. Proceed with the recipe as above.

A Tip from the Kitchen...

When serving warm cobbler-style and pudding-style desserts, scoop them into individual serving dishes and top with a fresh and contrasting topping, such as freshly whipped heavy cream, rich vanilla ice cream, cinnamon ice cream, or Crème Fraîche (see recipe on page 225). Sprinkle on toasted nuts, toasted macaroons, freshly grated coconut, or a crushed-up candy bar for texture and crunch. Perhaps add a slice of the fresh version of the dessert's fruit or even a contrasting fruit such as a slice of kiwi, fresh berries, or a sprig of mint. That little finishing touch can add the pizzazz that makes the ending of your meal memorable. Or maybe it's just presenting the dessert in pretty long-stemmed glasses instead of your everyday bowls. Make dessert special; give it your signature, your personal flair.

Bonnie's Stewed Rhubarb Compote

Makes 6 to 8 servings

- 4 to 5 cups sliced rhubarb, cut into 1-inch pieces
- 1 (0.3-ounce) package strawberry gelatin
- $2/3$ cup granulated sugar
- $1/3$ cup brown sugar
- 1 cup chopped pecans
- 2 tablespoons butter, for dotting
- Half-and-half, for serving

Spray the slow cooker with nonstick cooking spray. Place the rhubarb pieces in the slow cooker. Sprinkle on the gelatin and sugars evenly. Drizzle with ½ cup water. Sprinkle with the pecans evenly and dot with butter. Don't stir the mixture. Cover with the lid and cook on low for 2 to 4 hours, until the rhubarb is very soft and has released its juices. To serve, scoop warm or cold into dessert cups. Pass the half-and-half to pour over the compote.

—from the kitchen of Mike Gulan

Mixed Dried-Fruit Dessert Compote

Makes 8 servings

- 1 cup dried peach halves
- 1 cup dried apricot halves
- 1 cup dried apple slices
- ½ cup dried pineapple chunks
- ½ cup dried golden raisins
- ½ cup dried cranberries
- 4 teaspoons brown sugar
- Juice and 1 teaspoon grated zest from 1 lemon
- 2 teaspoons grated orange zest
- 1 (3 -inch) cinnamon stick
- 2 or 3 whole cloves
- 1 tablespoon brandy or orange liquor, or to taste (optional)
- Pound cake, sliced, for serving
- Vanilla ice cream, for serving

Mix the fruits and place them in the slow cooker. Sprinkle with the brown sugar, lemon juice, and both zests. Add 3 cups water, the cinnamon stick, and the cloves. Cover with the lid and cook on low for 6 to 7 hours, or until the fruits are tender. Stir in brandy or orange liqueur, if desired. Scoop the warm compote over individual slices of pound cake and top with rich vanilla ice cream.

Mocha Fondue

Makes 6 to 8 servings

Definitely not fat free, this is a sinful dessert for the chocolate lover!

- 20 ounces fine-quality milk chocolate, broken into pieces
- 1 cup heavy cream
- 1 to 2 tablespoons instant coffee or instant espresso powder, to taste
- Bite-sized pieces banana, pineapple, and angel food cake; donut holes; marshmallows; whole strawberries; or chunks of brownies, or similar dipping pieces, for serving.

Place chocolate pieces in the slow cooker and cook on high until the chocolate melts, stirring constantly. Reduce the heat to low. Stir in the heavy cream and coffee powder until smooth. Continue to keep warm on low while serving. Serve with dipping pieces. Skewer desired item on a fondue fork and dip into the warm fondue to coat. Eat immediately.

—from the kitchen of Wendy Louise

A Tip from the Kitchen...

Melting chocolate? Don't have room for a double boiler on the stove? Use your slow cooker!

The Rush Hour Cook's Fondue for You

- 1 (14-ounce) can condensed milk
- 1 cup semi-sweet chocolate chips
- Milk, if needed

Combine the condensed milk and chocolate in the slow cooker, stirring constantly until melted and smooth. Keep warm on low setting, for serving. Add milk to thin to desired consistency, if needed.

Serve as a dipping sauce for:

Strawberries

Graham crackers

Bananas

Marshmallows

Cantaloupe

Angel food cake

Ladyfingers

—*excerpted from* The Rush Hour Cook Presents Effortless Entertaining *by Brook Noel*

Dessert Dipped Strawberries

Makes 8 to 10 servings

- Fine-quality chocolate, for melting
- Choice fresh strawberries, left whole and stems on
- Waxed paper

Carefully melt the chocolate on low in the slow cooker. Dip the whole berries half to three-quarters of the way up in the chocolate. Lay in single layer on a cookie sheet lined with waxed paper and store in the refrigerator. The chocolate coating will set firm as it cools. Serve on doily-lined plates.

Cook's Note: You can also dip pretzels, coating them halfway into white or dark chocolate and using the exposed halves as handles. Store pretzels in airtight container once cooled.

—from the kitchen of Hannalorre

Mother's Bread Pudding

Makes 8 servings

- 6 cups cubed day-old or lightly toasted white bread
- 2 cups whole milk, scalded
- 4 tablespoons butter, melted in the scalding milk
- 1 cup raisins, dried tart cranberries, or dried cherries, plumped in the scalding milk
- 3 eggs, lightly beaten
- ½ cup granulated sugar
- 3 tablespoons brown sugar
- ¾ teaspoon ground cinnamon
- ¼ teaspoon ground nutmeg
- ¼ teaspoon salt
- 1 teaspoon vanilla extract
- Vanilla ice cream or half-and-half, for serving

Spray the slow cooker with non-stick cooking spray. Place the bread cubes in the cooker. Heat the milk with the butter and raisins until the butter melts and the milk is hot. Beat together the eggs, sugar, cinnamon, nutmeg, and salt. Add the milk mixture and mix until all is blended. Fold in the vanilla extract. Pour the mixture over the bread cubes. Let the pudding sit for 15 minutes so the bread can soak up the custard mixture. Cover with the lid and cook on high for 2½ to 3 hours, until a knife inserted in the center comes out clean.

Scoop the pudding into dessert bowls, and top with vanilla ice cream, or pass half-and-half to pour over the pudding. Serve warm.

—from the kitchen of Betty Tillman

June Wallace's Rice Pudding

Makes 8 dessert servings

Subtle, creamy—a true comfort food. Stir halfway through cooking; replace the lid, and continue cooking. It is important to not overlook this step. If serving the pudding cold, stir in ½ cup additional milk just before refrigerating pudding. Dust servings with cinnamon, if desired. Top with whipped cream or pour on half-and-half.

- 2 cups boiling water
- 1 cup Arborio rice
- ¼ teaspoon salt
- 3 cups milk, scalded
- ½ cup sugar
- ½ cup raisins, optional, plumped in water, rum, or orange juice
- 2 teaspoons vanilla extract
- ½ cup additional milk at end of cooking, if serving pudding cold

Spray the slow cooker with nonstick cooking spray. Place rice and salt in the slow cooker. Pour on the boiling water; stir. Cover with the lid and cook the rice on high for 1 hour. Stir in the warm milk and sugar. Replace the lid and cook on low for 2 to 3 hours more, until the rice is soft and the pudding is creamy. Stir in the plumped raisins, if using, and vanilla extract. Turn off the heat and let the pudding cool slightly before serving; serve warm.

—from the kitchen of June Wallace

The Story Lady's Sweet Caramel Custard

Makes 6 to 8 servings

- 4 medium eggs
- 1 teaspoon vanilla extract
- 3½ cups whole milk
- 4½ cups sugar, divided
- ½ cup boiling water
- Butter

Beat the eggs in a mixing bowl with an electric beater until thick. Add the vanilla and continue beating until lemon-colored. Add the milk and 2½ cups sugar; with the beater on low, continue mixing well. Set aside.

Butter a 2-quart mold and set aside. In a heavy, medium-sized skillet, melt the remaining 2 cups sugar over very low heat. When it begins to bubble and turn brown, stir to combine all the melting sugar in the skillet. When the caramelizing sugar is medium brown, pour half the caramelizing mixture into the bottom of the buttered mold; set aside. Into the other half of the caramelized sugar, pour the ½ cup boiling water, taking care to avoid splattering of the hot sugar. Continue to stir over low heat until the mixture bubbles again; allow it to cool, then chill for use as a sauce.

Now pour the beaten egg mixture (that you had set aside) into the buttered mold. Place a small trivet or rack in the bottom of the slow cooker, pour in 2 cups boiling water, and gently place the filled mold down into the water bath. Cover with the lid propped open just slightly to vent excess steam. Cook on high for 4 hours, until a knife inserted in the center of the custard comes out clean. When done, carefully remove the molded custard from the slow cooker and set aside to cool. Cover and chill. At serving time, invert and unmold. Serve with the reserved caramel sauce.

—from the kitchen of Bonnie Gulan

Kid's Favorite Hot Chocolate

Makes 8 servings

Put this on before you go out to enjoy a winter sport, and it will be waiting warm and toasty when you return home.

- 8 cups whole milk
- ½ cup granulated sugar
- 1 tablespoon brown sugar
- ⅔ cup chocolate syrup
- 1 teaspoon vanilla extract
- Mini-marshmallows, for serving
- Ground cinnamon, for serving

Mix together all ingredients, except the vanilla extract, and pour into the slow cooker. Cook on low for 2 to 3 hours, until thoroughly warm. Just before serving, stir in the vanilla extract. Ladle into mugs, and top with mini-marshmallows and/or a dusting of cinnamon, if desired.

Cook's Note: For Mocha-Flavored Hot Chocolate, stir 2 tablespoons instant coffee granules into the pot to dissolve completely.

Mulled Juice 'n Tea Punch

Makes 10 cups

- 1 quart cranberry juice
- 1 quart apple juice
- 1 (16- to 18-ounce) bottle or can tea with raspberry or pomegranate
- 4 to 6 whole cloves
- 1 to 3 (3–inch) cinnamon sticks, per your taste
- 2 whole black peppercorns
- 1 orange, thinly sliced, plus additional orange slices for garnish

Combine the two juices and tea in the slow cooker. Add the cloves, cinnamon stick, and peppercorns. Cover with the lid and cook on low for about 3 hours, until hot. Add the orange slices to the pot. Before serving, remove cinnamon stick, cloves, and peppercorns. Keep the punch on low while serving. Ladle into mugs, topping each serving with a fresh orange slice.

Mulled Wine

Makes 18 (5-ounce) servings

- ¾ cup granulated sugar
- 1 tablespoon brown sugar
- 2 (3-inch) cinnamon sticks
- 6 whole cloves
- 1 teaspoon ground allspice
- Peel from ½ lemon, cut into thin strips
- Peel from ½ orange, cut into thin strips
- 3 cups boiling water
- 2 (750-ml) bottles Burgundy wine
- Orange slices for garnish, if desired

Put all the ingredients, except the water and the wine, in the slow cooker. Pour the boiling water over top and let steep for 5 minutes. Pour the wine into the slow cooker. Cover with the lid and cook on high for 1 hour; reduce the heat to low and continue cooking until the mixture is heated through and the flavors have blended. Keep on low while serving. Serve warm in mugs. Garnish each with an orange slice, if desired.

Andy's Mulled Cider

Makes 8 to 10 servings

You can add brandy or rum into individual mugs at serving time, if you elect not to mull it in the punch itself.

- 1 (46-ounce) jug sweet apple cider
- Several cinnamon sticks
- Several whole cloves
- 1 cup brandy or rum (optional)
- 1 can lemon-flavored soda (optional)

Combine all the ingredients in slow cooker and bring to a simmer on high. Turn the heat to low and let the flavors "mull" for 2 hours. Serve warm.

—*from the kitchen of J. Andrew Stowers*

Dipped Jellied Candies

Let supervised youngsters enjoy making this treat.

- White chocolate, broken into chunks
- Large gum drops or jellied candy slices
- Toothpicks
- Waxed paper

Gently melt the white chocolate in the slow cooker, stirring constantly. Using toothpicks, spear the candy, and submerge into the melted white chocolate to coat. Transfer to waxed paper and let coating cool. Remove the toothpicks and store in an airtight container.

—from the kitchen of Robin Sabatke

Recipe Index

About the Author

A Wisconsin resident, Wendy Louise currently lives near her daughter, son-in-law, and granddaughter. When she is not busy pursuing life-long interests in the fine arts, quilting, crafting, and gardening, she turns her interest to cooking and sharing in the family dinner hour. She believes that enjoying good food is one of the finer pleasures in life and that eating well is an important element toward attaining family comfort and well-being.